An Introduction to Dynamic Data Stru

An Introduction to Dynamic Data Structures

Raymond Wilson

Lecturer in Computer Science
Teesside Polytechnic

McGRAW-HILL BOOK COMPANY

London · New York · St Louis · San Francisco · Auckland · Bogotá
Guatemala · Hamburg · Lisbon · Madrid · Mexico · Montreal · New Delhi
Panama · Paris · San Juan · São Paulo · Singapore · Sydney · Tokyo · Toronto

Published by
McGRAW-HILL Book Company (UK) Limited
MAIDENHEAD · BERKSHIRE · ENGLAND

British Library Cataloguing in Publication Data

Wilson, Raymond
   Introduction to dynamic data structures.
   1. Computer systems. Structured programming.
   Programming languages.: Pascal language
   I. Title
   005.13′3

   ISBN 0-07-084188-8

Library of Congress Cataloging-in-Publication Data

Wilson, Raymond.
   An introduction to dynamic data structures/Raymond Wilson.
     p.   cm.
   Bibliography: p.
   Includes index.
   ISBN 0-07-084188-8
   1. Data structures (Computer science) I. Title
  QA76.9.D35W54   1988   88-2751
  005.7′3--dc19

1234CUP 898
Typeset by Advanced Filmsetters (Glasgow) Ltd
and printed and bound at the University Press, Cambridge

*Dedicated to my family
and to
Colin Geoffrey Kendray*

Contents

Preface   xi

Part One

1	MEMORY ORGANIZATION	3
1.1	Introduction	3
1.2	Data storage	3
1.3	Algorithm 1. Getting a node from the pool	9
1.4	Algorithm 2. Returning an unwanted node	10
1.5	Algorithm 3. Initializing the general storage pool	12

2	BUILDING LINEAR DATA STRUCTURES	15
2.1	Algorithm 4. Building a linked list	15
2.2	Algorithm 5. Writing out the contents of a linked list	18
2.3	Program 1	18
2.4	Linked list searches	18
2.5	Recursion in lists	19
2.6	Algorithm 6. Searching a linked list for a given node	22
2.7	Program 2	23
2.8	Adding nodes to an existing linked list	23
2.9	Algorithm 7. Inserting a node between existing nodes	23
2.10	Removing a node from a linked list	24
2.11	Algorithm 8. Deletion of a node	24
2.12	Special cases of node insertion	25
2.13	Algorithm 9. General node insertion	25
2.14	Algorithm 10. General node deletion	26
2.15	An ordered linked list	28
2.16	Algorithm 11. Building an ordered list	28
2.17	Sentinal nodes	28
2.18	Program 3	30
2.19	Problem set 1	31

3	SOME APPLICATIONS OF LINKED LISTS	34
3.1	The queue	34
3.2	The barbers' shop. A simple example of modelling a queue	34
3.3	Algorithm 12. A simple queue simulation	35

3.4   Algorithm 13. Joining a queue   36
3.5   Algorithm 14. Servicing a customer   36
3.6   Program 4   37
3.7   The stack   38
3.8   Using a stack to change number bases   41
3.9   Algorithm 15. The number base problem   41
3.10   Program 5   42
3.11   An application of stacks to the evaluation of arithmetic
       expressions   42
3.12   Algorithm 16. Stack evaluation   43
3.13   Program 6   44
3.14   Using linked lists for the storage of sparse arrays   44
3.15   Further list processing. List builder and selector functions   47
3.16   Algorithm 17. Reversing the nodes in a linked list   49
3.17   Using linked lists to represent sets of objects   50
3.18   Set intersection   51
3.19   Algorithm 18. Intersection of two ordered sets   51
3.20   Set union   52
3.21   Algorithm 19. The union of two ordered sets   53
3.22   Membership of a set   55
3.23   Equality of two ordered sets   55
3.24   Set inclusion   56
3.25   Set difference   57
3.26   Algorithm 20. The difference of two ordered sets   57
3.27   Program 7   58
3.28   Complex list structures   59
3.29   The library problem   61
3.30   Program 8   62
3.31   Problem set 2   62

4   NON-LINEAR DATA STRUCTURES   70
4.1   Trees   70
4.2   Binary trees   72
4.3   Tree representation in computer memory   73
4.4   Program 9   76
4.5   Searching a binary tree   76
4.6   Inserting a node into a binary tree   76
4.7   Deletion of a node from a binary tree   78
4.8   Tree traversals   82
4.9   Algorithm 21. An in-order tree traversal   83
4.10   Algorithm 22. A pre-order traversal   86
4.11   Algorithm 23. A post-order traversal   89
4.12   Program 10   89
4.13   Graphs and linked lists   92

4.14   Representation of a directed graph in computer memory   93
4.15   Partial orderings   96
4.16   Algorithm 24. A topological sort   97
4.17   Program 11   101
4.18   Paths through a graph   102
4.19   A building project   103
4.20   A travel problem   105
4.21   Program 12   110
4.22   Problem set 3   110

Part Two

5   AN INTRODUCTION TO LANGUAGE DEFINITION   117
5.1   A language generator   117
5.2   A grammar as a language generator mechanism   118
5.3   Representing a grammar in computer memory   118
5.4   Algorithm 25. A sentence generator   121
5.5   Program 13   122
5.6   Derivation trees   122
5.7   The language of simple expressions   125
5.8   An ambiguous grammar   127
5.9   Syntax graphs   128
5.10   A syntax analyser   130
5.11   Program 14   131
5.12   Expression trees   131
5.13   The notation of simple expressions   132
5.14   Traversals of expression trees   134
5.15   Building expression trees   135
5.16   Program 15   139
5.17   Problem set 4   139

6   EVALUATION OF EXPRESSIONS   142
6.1   Evaluation machines   144
6.2   Algorithm 26. Code generation for a stack machine   146
6.3   Program 16   146
6.4   Code generation for a register-based machine   146
6.5   Program 17   152
6.6   Reordering of expressions   152
6.7   Tree transformation   154
6.8   Algorithm 27. Transforming a tree   154
6.9   Algorithm 28. Use of reverse operators   158
6.10   Program 18   159

7   A COMPLETE EXPRESSION EVALUATION SYSTEM   160
7.1   The interpretive system   161
7.2   Program 19   162

7.3   The compiled system   163
7.4   Program 20   165

Part Three
      Partial listings relating to the programs throughout the book 167

Glossary   230

Index   237

Preface

Why dynamic data structures?

Quite often we write computer programs in which we represent dynamic situations. Take as an example a simple ordered list of names of people: the list can grow as names are added and decrease as names are deleted. If a static data structure, such as an array, is used to represent the list of names, it must be big enough to contain all possible additions. This can lead to an initial over-estimation of the array size and a waste of computer memory. If, on the other hand, we underestimate the array size required, we can find the array is soon full and no more names can be added.

With a dynamic data structure we add storage only as it is required and in the case of deletions we can return unwanted storage for re-use. The availability of dynamic data structures to model dynamic situations can save on storage and often allows a more structured approach to programming.

The book is divided into three parts:

Part One (Chapters 1 to 4) introduces the concept of dynamic data storage, together with the building of dynamic data structures. These are deliberately restricted to simple linked lists and binary trees.

Part Two (Chapters 5 to 7) starts with an introduction to language definition. A language for simple algebraic expressions is defined which is then used as a vehicle for illustrating the application of dynamic data structures to some problems generally associated with compiler construction.

Part Three contains partial listings of the programs referred to in the book. Each listing consists of the names of the necessary procedures/functions together with the main program segment. The programs are meant to be illustrative only and as such do not provide rigorous data validation procedures, etc. Input data is assumed to be correct.

The reader should note, however, that some of the Pascal programs given in the text do not use DISPOSE to return used dynamic storage to the Pascal pool. Including this function would have led to greater complexity, for this reason I have sometimes chosen to omit it.

It is hoped that this book will provide a useful introductory text for any student embarking on a computer science course in higher education. As well as being a study in its own right it will also act as a supplement to many programming textbooks.

All of the programming examples are written in standard Pascal.

Finally, I should like to acknowledge the help that I have received from my colleague Ken Hanford and from my son Richard.

Raymond Wilson

PART ONE

Introduction to the concept of
dynamic data structures

1
Memory organization

1.1 Introduction

The object of this book is to introduce the reader to the concept of dynamic structures. Most of the ideas contained in the book are amplified by simple application programs for the reader to study.

It is hoped that in the following pages the advantages of using such structures in certain situations will be seen and appreciated together with their influence on the creation of algorithms.

1.2 Data storage

In all computer systems there are facilities provided for storing data. The simplest of these is the single 'storage box' which is referenced by a name (identifier). These names are simply substitutes for actual memory addresses and are used to identify locations in the computer's memory. In systems running the language BASIC such storage boxes are allocated when new identifiers are encountered in the program.

$$1 \text{ LET } X = 5$$
$$2 \text{ LET } Y = 6$$
$$3 \text{ PRINT } X + Y$$

In the above program, the execution of lines 1 and 2 cause storage boxes, referenced by the identifiers X and Y, to be allocated. The integers 5 and 6 are then stored in these boxes. This can be illustrated as shown in Fig. 1.1.

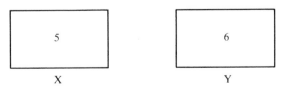

Figure 1.1 Data storage 'boxes'

Whenever the identifiers X and Y are used in the program they refer to the contents of the memory locations they reference (or point to). These contents are normally termed the values of X and Y. At a later stage in the program these initial values may be changed; e.g.

$$\text{Let } X = X + 1$$

Hence they are termed variable identifiers or just variables. In other languages the process of reserving single data storage boxes is slightly more complex. In the language Pascal, for instance, all such storage boxes must be allocated before they can be used. The following segment of Pascal illustrates how this is accomplished:

var a,b:integer;

The storage boxes a and b are allocated but at this point their contents are undefined. Furthermore, when these storage boxes are assigned contents, those contents are restricted to integer values. For example, the results of 1.2 multiplied by 3.6 could not be stored in either of the boxes referenced by a or b as it is a real number. Hence it can be seen that in Pascal the type of data being stored is dealt with more rigorously. When, say, one thousand data items (all of the same type) need to be stored, it would appear that one thousand different identifiers need to be declared. This is, to say the least, very impracticable and so a more practical data storage structure is needed. The simplest type of data structure that can cope with this sort of storage problem is known as a storage vector or a one-dimensional *array*. This is simply a set of single storage boxes referred to by one identifier. An array is shown in Fig. 1.2.

Here the array identifier is x and refers to the ten storage boxes as a complete unit or structure. In order to access a particular box or array element, the use of subscript or index notation is invoked. Thus x[1] refers to the leftmost element while x[10] refers to the rightmost element. Obviously the storage boxes must occupy contiguous locations in memory in order to make access to any array element possible using the index notation. The number of elements an array contains must be decided at the beginning of a program, and in Pascal this is done as follows:

var x:array[1 .. n]of integer;

This statement allocates storage boxes indexed by the integers 1 to n and further states that each box can only ever contain an integer value. Assignments to these

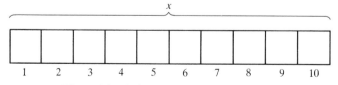

Figure 1.2   A simple one-dimensional array

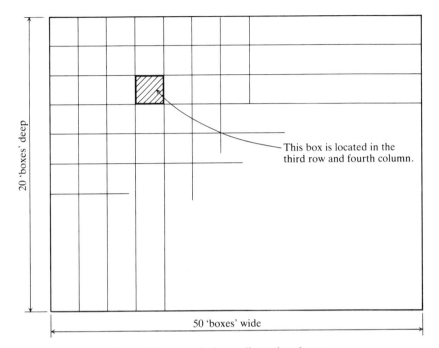

Figure 1.3 A typical two-dimensional array

boxes can now be made using the index notation; e.g.

$$x[3] := 5;$$

$$x[n] := 10;$$

These assignments place the integer 5 in the third box and the integer 10 in the *n*th box.

Arrays can be multidimensional. It may sometimes be more convenient to save a set of data items in a matrix or two-dimensional array. An array such as that shown in Fig. 1.3 is declared as follows:

$$var\ twodim[1..20, 1..50] of\ integer;$$

To access a single element of this array now requires the use of a double subscript or index.

The assignment statement

$$twodim[5, 10] := 25;$$

identifies the box in the fifth row and in the tenth column. The reader can no doubt imagine uses for such data structures, e.g. grid referencing problems, table manipulations, etc.

As with all data structures there is always some trade-off between the

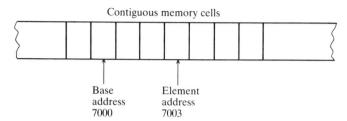

Figure 1.4 Sequential allocation of memory for storing elements of a one-dimensional array

advantage of using a particular data structure and element manipulation times. In order to access indexed elements of a one-dimensional array the system needs to know the memory address of the first element; then by using the index value, it can calculate the address of the specified array element. Thus, if the starting or base address of an array is given as 7000, the address of the fourth element is 7003 (Fig. 1.4).

In the case of a two-dimensional array, calculating the address of a particular element is a little more difficult. If the array is assumed to be stored by rows as shown in Fig. 1.5, then using the array base address together with the first subscript for a given element the address of the row in which the given element resides can be calculated. Once the start of the row address is known it is easy to locate the specified element in that row by means of the second subscript.

One method of calculating an array element address in this way is to use a mapping function. Given the start or base address of any array as BA and assuming the array is stored by rows, the following mapping functions could be used.

For a one-dimensional array, declared as follows:

$$\text{var x:array}[1\,..\,n]\text{of integer};$$

the address for the general element i is given by the function

$$M(i) = BA + i - 1$$

For a two-dimensional array declared as follows:

$$\text{var x:array}[1\,..\,m, 1\,..\,n];$$

the address for the general element (i,j) is given by the function

$$M(i,j) = BA + n(i-1) + j - 1$$

One of the disadvantages of arrays is that in many languages each 'box' can only contain data items that are basic or simple types. This, however, is not true of all languages; in Pascal, for instance, arrays can contain complex data items. One such complex data item is the *record*. A record is a data type that allows mixed types of data to be held as a unit. It can be pictured as a 'box'

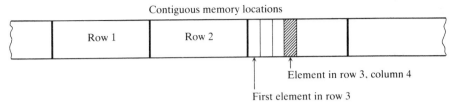

Figure 1.5   Sequential allocation of memory for storing elements of a two-dimensional array

Field identifier	Field contents
name	
age	
tel	
sex	

Figure 1.6   A typical record

with subdivisions where each subdivision can contain data of differing types (see Fig. 1.6).

Each subdivision or *field* is identified by a unique name. Such a record type as illustrated is defined as follows. The record has the typename, *person*.

```
type person = record
              name:packed array[1..6]of char;
              age   :integer;
              tel   :integer;
              sex   :char
            end;
```

The fields of records may contain simple or base types or more complex types such as arrays or even other records.

If a variable of type person is declared, the complete record is referenced by this variable; e.g.

var self:person;

In order to access the different fields of a record use is made of the *dot* notation. Thus

self.name

gives access to the name field, while

self.tel

gives access to the field containing the telephone number. These 'dotted' variables can be used in suitable statements in the same way normal variables are used; e.g.

> self.name := 'WILSON';
> self.tel := 817718;
> if self.name = 'SMITH' then......
> While self.age⟨40 do......
> Writeln(self.sex);

With the availability of records, new types can be introduced into programs to suit the data being processed. If the same information about each person in a class of students is required, an array of records can be used:

> class : array[1..50]of person;

Access to the name of the kth person in the class is achieved as follows:

> class[k].name

It can be seen that using records in this way allows very complex data structures to be designed. However, it must be noted that such arrays still only provide *static* data structures. An alternative method for storing sets of data items held in records is to use a *linked* or *dynamic* storage system. Each element, instead of appearing sequentially between its predecessor and successor, is linked to its successor and therefore contiguous storage locations are not necessary.

In sequential storage, as already mentioned, any element can be addressed directly by the use of subscript notation (see Fig. 1.7).

In linked storage each element contains a *link* to its successor. This link is in actual fact just the store or memory address of the successor element and the last or end element contains a special address (the *nil* link) to indicate that it has no successor. It must be noted that using the linked storage method, system overheads are incurred by the storing and accessing of links.

In a linked storage scheme elements can only be accessed through the head or main link; thus by starting with the head link and following down the chain of links all of the elements can be accessed (Fig. 1.8). Elements of linked storage systems are often called *nodes* and in their simplest form consist of two *fields*, a *data* field to hold information and a *link* field to hold the address of the successor node (Fig. 1.9).

In order to implement and build data structures using nodes as described, it is necessary to have available a general pool of storage from which nodes can be

M_1 M_2 M_3 M_4 .   .   . M_n

Figure 1.7   Sequential memory allocation for array elements

Head or main link

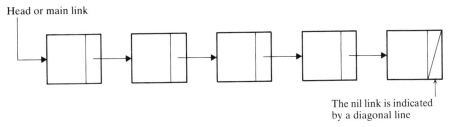

The nil link is indicated
by a diagonal line

Figure 1.8   A linked storage system

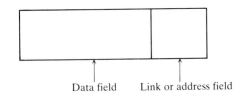

Data field   Link or address field

Figure 1.9   A typical node

Freehead

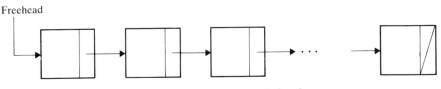

Figure 1.10   A general pool of nodes

obtained when required and to which nodes can be returned when no longer needed. This general pool of storage can be thought of as a linked storage system such as that shown in Fig. 1.10.

To get a node when required from this storage pool we remove the head node. This is accomplished by resetting the freehead address. It would be helpful to think of linked addresses as *pointers* to the nodes they address. However, once a node has been removed from the pool, we need to keep a reference to its address and we do this by means of a pointer variable. In Algorithms 1, 2 and 3 this pointer variable is called *newnode*. Other pointer variables used in these algorithms are *freehead*, *oldnode* and *listhead*.

1.3   Algorithm 1. Getting a node from the pool

Getanewnode
begin
  Set newnode to freehead
  Set freehead to link field of node pointed to by freehead
end

Application of Algorithm 1 changes the picture of the general storage pool, as shown in Fig. 1.11.

In Algorithm 1 we assume that an unlimited supply of nodes is available. In practice, however, when a new node is needed the storage pool must first be checked to make sure that it is not empty.

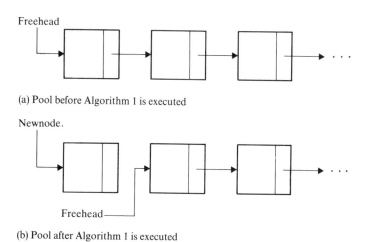

(a) Pool before Algorithm 1 is executed

(b) Pool after Algorithm 1 is executed

Figure 1.11   Getting a node from the general pool

1.4   Algorithm 2. Returning an unwanted node

Returnanoldnode
begin
    Set link field of oldnode to freehead
    Set freehead to oldnode
end

Application of Algorithm 2 changes the picture of the general storage pool as shown in Fig. 1.12.

From the foregoing it can be seen that a dynamic storage mechanism is created, nodes being created as required and then returned to the general pool when finished with. In some microcomputers this dynamic storage mechanism can be implemented by directly addressing the hardware random access memory. However, to simplify programming, the sequential hardware random access memory can be modelled by the sequential structure of arrays as shown in Fig. 1.13. This allows the programmer to simulate dynamic storage together with its use in a limited sort of way.

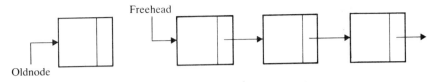

(a) Pool before Algorithm 2 is executed

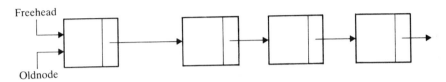

(b) Pool after Algorithm 2 is executed

Figure 1.12 Returning a node to the general pool

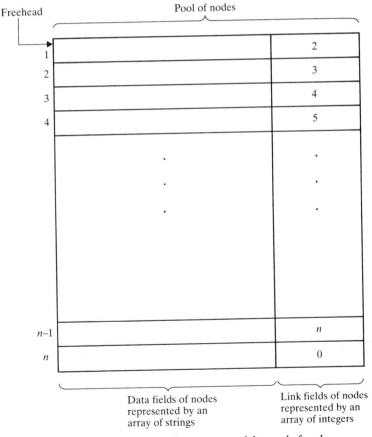

Figure 1.13 The use of arrays to model a pool of nodes

1.5 Algorithm 3. Initializing the general storage pool

```
Initializepool
begin
    dimension arrays representing data and link fields
    set freehead to point to first array element
    link each element to its successor
    put nil link in end element
end
```

In Algorithm 3 we assume that data fields of nodes will contain single or multicharacter strings and link fields will contain integer addresses (pointers). The following procedures, written in a form of structured BASIC, implement Algorithms 1, 2 and 3:

```
1  DEF PROCgetnewnode
2      newnode = freehead
3      freehead = link(freehead)
4  ENDPROC
```

```
1  DEF PROCputoldnode
2      link(oldnode) = freehead
3      freehead = oldnode
4  ENDPROC
```

```
1  DEF PROCinitfreelist
2      size = 100
3      DIM data$(size),link(size)
4      freehead = 1
5      for i = 1 TO size − 1
6          link(i) = i + 1
7      NEXT i
8      link(size) = 0
9  ENDPROC
```

In the programming language Pascal there is no need for this kind of simulation as the necessary mechanisms for creating nodes dynamically are provided. The Pascal functions *new* and *dispose* enable the programmer to get and return nodes from or to the storage pool. These nodes or variables, because they can be created and disposed of anywhere in the program, are known as *dynamic variables*. In Pascal implementations, this storage pool is called the *heap*. To use the new and dispose functions the following types need to be defined:

1. A pointer to a node
2. The type of node pointed to

This is done as follows:

```
type link = ↑node;     {a pointer to a node}
      node = record     {a node}
                  data:integer;
                  next:link
            end;
```

It can be seen that the second type of definition defines a record that has two fields identified by the names 'data' and 'next'. Figure 1.14 illustrates such a record.

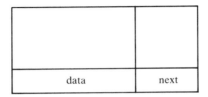

Figure 1.14   A record modelling a simple node

The 'data' field can contain integer values and the 'next' field can contain a pointer. This pointer may have a nil value or may point to another node, in this case, of the same type. The following segment of Pascal illustrates the aquisition of such a node from the heap and also the way that values are assigned to its fields:

```
var x:link;
begin
    NEW(x);
    x↑.data:= 5;
    x↑.next:= NIL
end;
```

The variable x is a static variable which is of type LINK and therefore may contain a pointer to a dynamic variable of type NODE. After the execution of NEW(x) the situation as shown in Fig. 1.15 is created.

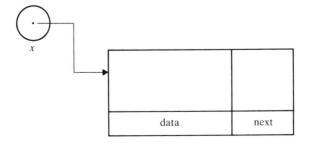

Figure 1.15   Creating a new mode of a given type

To access the fields of a node it can be seen that the *dot* notation is used; i.e.

$$x\uparrow.data$$

identifies the node pointed to by x and the field labelled data while

$$x\uparrow.next$$

identifies the node pointed to by x and the field labelled next. To return an unwanted node to the general storage pool the function DISPOSE is used. Thus

$$DISPOSE(x)$$

returns to the heap, the node pointed to by x.

2
Building linear data structures

A simple *linked list* (Fig. 2.1) consists of a set of nodes linked together with a special pointer to the first or *head* node. The data fields of each node contain some sort of information and the end of the list is signalled by a node containing the nil pointer.

We now examine the following algorithm which builds such a list.

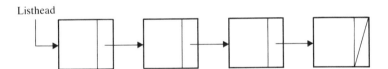

Listhead

Figure 2.1   A simple linked list

2.1   Algorithm 4. Building a linked list

```
Buildalistinreverseorder
begin
    set the pointer variable listhead to contain
        a nil pointer
    while still input do
    begin
        get a new node from the storage pool
        enter data into data field of node
        set link field of node to value in listhead
        set listhead to point at new node
    end
end
```

Given that the items of data are three single characters A, B and C, we can follow through the working of the algorithm as follows:

Step	Action	

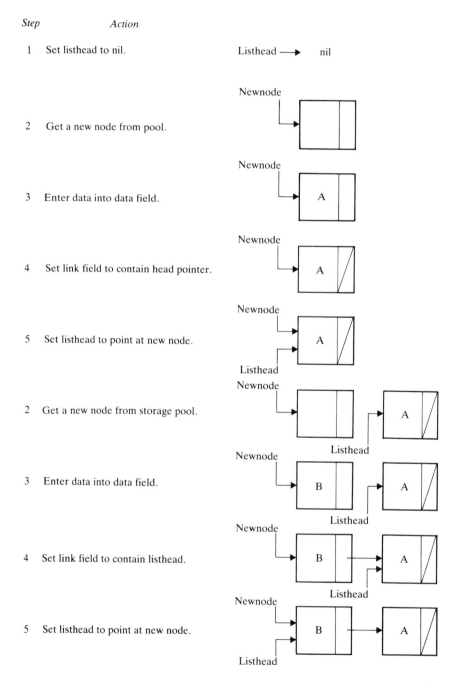

1	Set listhead to nil.	Listhead ⟶ nil
2	Get a new node from pool.	
3	Enter data into data field.	
4	Set link field to contain head pointer.	
5	Set listhead to point at new node.	
2	Get a new node from storage pool.	
3	Enter data into data field.	
4	Set link field to contain listhead.	
5	Set listhead to point at new node.	

Repeating steps 2, 3, 4 and 5 once again completes the building of the list as shown in Fig. 2.2.

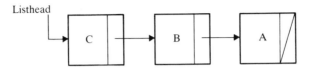

Figure 2.2 The completed list as built by Algorithm 4

Notice how the list has been constructed in the reverse order of the input. At this stage it is convenient to use this method as it is the easiest way of constructing a linked list.

A procedure to implement Algorithm 4 is given below. This procedure makes repeated use of the system function NEW and terminates when the input reads the character '?'.

Assuming the global declarations:

```
type link = ↑node;
     node = record
                 data:char;
                 next:link
            end;
var listhead:link;
```

```
procedure BUILDALISTINREVERSE(var ptr:link);
var ch:char;
    temp:link;
begin
  ptr:= nil;
  readln(ch);
  while ch⟨⟩'?' do
  begin
    new(temp);
    temp↑.data := ch;
    temp↑.next := ptr;
    ptr:= temp;
    readln(ch)
  end
end;
```

Having built a list in computer memory we can check that it is correct by printing out the contents of the data field of each node. This is achieved by the following algorithm.

2.2   Algorithm 5. Writing out the contents of a linked list

```
Writealist(pointer)
begin
    repeat
        print data field of node pointed at by pointer
        move pointer to successor node
    until end of list is reached
end
```

Algorithm 5 is implemented by the following procedure, which when called has passed to it, as a value parameter, a pointer to the first node of the list, generally referred to as the head-of-list pointer:

```
procedure WRITEALIST(ptr:link);
begin
    while ptr<>nil do
    begin
        writeln(ptr↑.data);
        ptr:= ptr↑.next
    end
end;
```

2.3   Program 1*

Using the procedures given, this program builds a linked list as described and prints out its contents. Each data item is a single character and input is terminated by the character '?'.

2.4   Linked list searches

Quite often we need to search a linked list in order to find out if a given item of data is present or not. The reasons for this search could be one of the following:

1. To delete a given node from the list
2. To insert a new node at a particular point in the list
3. To collect information from the secondary fields of a node

Before considering a suitable search algorithm we introduce the concept of a list *tail*.

A linked list, as we have already seen, has a special node called the head node. We now define all successor nodes to this head node as the list tail (Fig. 2.3).

Thus a linked list consists of a head and a tail. Furthermore, we can think of

---

* Partial listings of the programs referred to throughout the book are to be found in Part Three, pages 169 to 229.

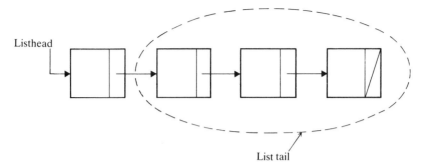

Figure 2.3 The concept of a list head and tail

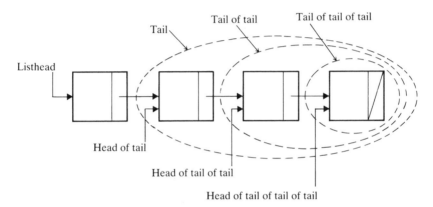

Figure 2.4 The concept of lists within lists

the tail of a list also as a list (see Fig. 2.4). Thus tails can be thought of as lists, each with a head and a tail. We define a list consisting of just a single node as a list with an empty tail.

2.5 Recursion in lists

Before continuing with our list operations we introduce the concept of recursion and recursive algorithms.

A recursive definition is such that the item being defined is defined in terms of itself.

To define our ancestors we could say that:

Our ancestors are our parents, our parents' parents, our parents' parents' parents,..., and so on.

Defining our ancestors recursively we say:

Our ancestors are our parents and our parents' ancestors.

In arithmetic we could define an integer as follows:

An integer is a digit, or a digit followed by a digit, or a digit followed by a digit, ..., and so on.

Using a recursive definition we say:

An integer is a digit or an integer followed by a digit.

Returning to our lists for a moment, we have just seen that a list consists of a head and a tail and that a tail consists of a head and a tail, and so on.... . Using recursion we can define a list thus:

A list is a head followed by a list.

A data structure that can be defined in this way is known as a recursive data structure. When solving problems involving such data structures it is often convenient to make use of recursive algorithms.

Before turning to the design of recursive algorithms for use with lists we first examine two examples from mathematics.

FINDING THE SUM OF THE FIRST n INTEGERS

The sum

$$1+2+3+4+\cdots+n$$

can be defined as

$$[1+2+3+4+\cdots+(n-1)]+n$$

From this we can see that the sum of the first n integers is the sum of the first $(n-1)$ integers plus n. Also, if $n = 1$ the sum is 1.

Mathematically we can define this sum by the equations

$$F(1) = 1$$
$$F(n) = F(n-1)+n \qquad (n > 1)$$

Writing this solution as a function in a pseudo programming language we have

$$\text{Sum (n)} = \text{if n} = 1 \text{ then 1 else Sum(n}-1)+\text{n}$$

Following through the recursive calls of this function for an initial value of $n = 3$ should help in understanding how it works (see Fig. 2.5).

THE FIBONACCI NUMBERS

The Fibonacci numbers are the numbers of the infinite sequence

$$1\ 1\ 2\ 3\ 5\ 8\ 13\ 21\ldots$$

such that each number, except for the first and second, is the sum of its two

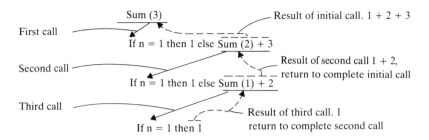

Figure 2.5   An illustration of calls on a recursive function

immediate predecessors. As before, we can define this sequence by the use of equations as follows:

$$F(1) = 1$$
$$F(2) = 1$$
$$F(n) = F(n-1) + F(n-2) \qquad (n > = 2)$$

Again using a pseudo programming language we can design a recursive function which returns the nth Fibonacci number:

$$\text{FIB(n)} = \text{if n} = 1 \text{ then } 1$$
$$\text{else if n} = 2 \text{ then } 1$$
$$\text{else FIB(n}-1) + \text{FIB(n}-2)$$

Following the calls of this function for an initial value of $n = 3$ helps in understanding how it works (see Fig. 2.6).

Returning to our lists we now apply the concept of recursion to the problem of calculating the number of nodes in any given list. Referring to Fig. 2.4 we can see that the number of nodes in a list is given by the number of nodes in its tail plus one. Also, if the pointer variable listhead contains a nil pointer, there are zero nodes in the list. Thus we implement a function which returns the length of a list as follows:

```
Function LENGTH(ptr:link):integer;
begin
  if ptr = nil then length:= 0
  else
  length:= length(ptr↑.next)+1
end;
```

This is analogous to the sum of the first n integers and the reader should be able to trace the history of function calls in a similar manner.

We now return to the problem of searching a linked list for the contents of a given node and give as one possible solution the following recursive algorithm.

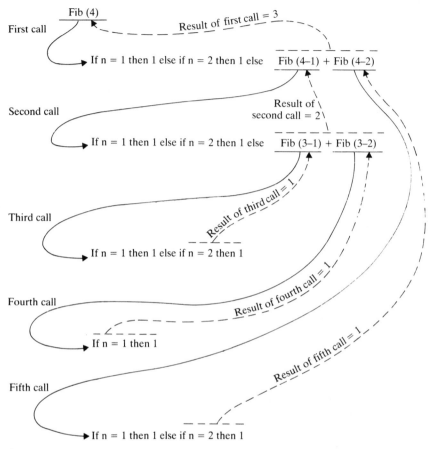

Figure 2.6 An illustration of calls on the Fibonacci function involving double recursion

2.6 Algorithm 6. Searching a linked list for a given node

                Search (list,item)
                begin
                    if list is empty then item is not present
                    else
                    if head contains item then item found
                    else
                    Search (tail of list,item)
                end

If you are not quite sure how this algorithm works it simply searches by
examining the head, the head of the tail, the head of the tail of the tail, etc., until
either a match is found or the list ends. We now define a procedure to implement
this algorithm.

```
procedure SEARCHLIST(ptr:link;item:char);
begin
  if ptr = nil then writeln('Item not in list')
  else
  if ptr↑.data = item then writeln('Item found')
  else
    searchlist(ptr↑.next,item)
end;
```

2.7 Program 2

This program builds a linked list subject to the same restrictions as imposed by Program 1. When the list is completed you are invited to enter a search item (a single character). The search procedure is invoked and the list searched for an occurrence of the search item.

2.8 Adding nodes to an existing linked list

One of the advantages of linked lists is the comparative ease with which new nodes can be inserted. To insert a node *between* two existing nodes merely requires resetting the pointer values in the link fields of nodes rather than having to move around a lot of data, as would be the case if arrays were used. Suppose we have a list as shown in Fig. 2.7 where the information in each node is the name of a person.

If we wish to insert a node containing the name CHARLIE *between* the nodes containing the names BILL and DAVID, we proceed as outlined in the following algorithm.

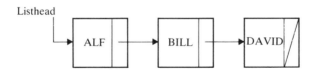

Figure 2.7   The linked list of names used to illustrate node insertion

2.9 Algorithm 7. Inserting a node between existing nodes

```
Insert
begin
  get a new node from the pool
  set data field of new node to contain CHARLIE
  set link field of new node to point at node containing DAVID
  set link field of BILL to point at new node
end
```

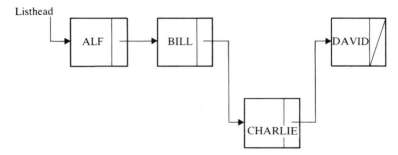

Figure 2.8   Insertion of a new node containing the name CHARLIE

Application of this algorithm changes the list as shown in Fig. 2.8.

Thus when following down the chain of links the node containing the name CHARLIE is found in its expected position.

2.10   Removing a node from a linked list

Deletion of a given node from *between* two nodes is even easier than insertion, as only one pointer value needs to be changed. As before, suppose we have a list of nodes each containing the name of a person, as shown in Fig. 2.9.

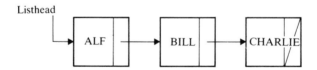

Figure 2.9   The linked list of names used to illustrate node deletion

Now suppose we wish to delete the node containing the name BILL from the list.

2.11   Algorithm 8. Deletion of a node

> delete
> begin
>   set the variable oldnode to point at BILL
>   set link field of ALF to point at node containing CHARLIE
>   return oldnode to storage pool
> end

Figure 2.10 shows the list after the application of the delete algorithm and as before, following down the chain of links, we see that the node containing the name CHARLIE is now the successor node to the node containing ALF, the node containing BILL having been removed from the list.

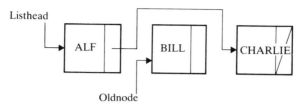

Figure 2.10 Deletion of a node containing the name BILL

2.12 Special cases of node insertion

Algorithm 7 deals with the insertion of a new node *between* existing nodes in a list. However, when the new node is to be inserted as the predecessor to the head node or as the successor to the end node, we have a special situation to consider. To help with these special cases we introduce two new ideas, the *end-of-list* pointer and the *ordered list*. By the term ordered list we mean that there exists some order relation between the items of data in each node. For the purpose of this text the order relation used is the character collating sequence order. Thus we say that A comes *before* B and X comes *after* C. Figure 2.11 shows such an ordered list (we will deal with the problem of building ordered lists later in the text).

A revised version of Algorithm 7 is now given.

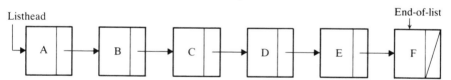

Figure 2.11 An ordered linked list

2.13 Algorithm 9. General node insertion

generalnodeinsertion
begin
   if the list is empty or the new node comes before
      the current head node then insert the new node
      as the head node
   else
   if the new node comes after the end node then
      insert the new node as the end node
   else
      insert the new node in the body of the list
end

Similar arguments apply to the deletion algorithm and a revised version of this is now given.

2.14   Algorithm 10. General node deletion

```
generalnodedeletion
begin
   if the list is empty then node cannot be deleted
   else
   if node to be deleted is head node then create a new head
   else
   delete node from tail of list
end
```

There is a need to search an ordered list to find out the position for insertion or deletion; this is taken care of in the following implementations of Algorithms 9 and 10:

```
procedure SEARCHANDINSERT(var ptr:link;item:char);
var temp,search:link;
   inserted:boolean;
begin
   new(temp);
   temp↑.data : = item;
   temp↑.next : = nil;
   search : = ptr;
   inserted : = false;
   if ptr = nil then
   begin
      ptr : = temp;
      endptr : = temp
   end
   else
   if item⟨ptr↑.data then
   begin
      temp↑.next : = ptr;
      ptr : = temp
   end
   else
   if item ⟩endptr↑.data then
   begin
      endptr↑.next : = temp;
      endptr : = temp
   end
   else
   repeat
      if(item⟩ = search↑.data)and(item⟨ = search↑.next↑.data)then
```

```
      begin
        temp↑.next : = search↑.next;
        search↑.next : = temp;
        inserted : = true
      end
      else
        search : = search↑.next
      until inserted
    end;
```

The procedure takes, as actual parameters, the head-of-list pointer and the data item to be inserted.

The reader should dry-run through this procedure to make sure that it is clearly understood. The following procedure implements the amended deletion algorithm:

```
    procedure SEARCHANDDELETE(var ptr:link;item:char);
    var search1,search2:link;
    begin
      search1 : = ptr;
      if search1 = nil then writeln('List is empty')
      else
      if search1↑.data = item then
      begin
        ptr : = search1↑.next;
        dispose(search1)
      end
      else
      begin
        while(search1↑.next⟨ ⟩nil)and(search1↑.data⟨ ⟩item)do
        begin
          search2 : = search1;
          search1 : = search1↑.next
        end;
        if search1↑.data = item then
        begin
          search2↑.next : = search1↑.next;
          if search1 = endptr then endptr : = search2;
          dispose(search1)
        end
        else
        writeln('Item not in list')
      end
    end;
```

This procedure makes use of two pointers to search through the list. The pointer called search1 is used to find the item in the list while the pointer called search2 follows one node behind. Thus when the item to be deleted is found, search2 is used to reset the necessary links.

2.15   An ordered linked list

Earlier in the text we assumed the existence of an ordered linked list. However, our original list building procedure (see Section 2.1) simply builds a list in the reverse order of the input stream. Replacing calls on this procedure with repetitive calls on our new search-and-insert procedure will build a list which is ordered, as search-and-insert always inserts nodes into their correct position with respect to the ordering constraints given.

2.16   Algorithm 11.   Building an ordered list

```
buildanorderedlist
begin
    initialize an empty list
    repeat
        insert items into list in order
    until all items inserted
end
```

The following procedure implements Algorithm 11:

```
procedure BUILDORDEREDLIST(var ptr:link);
begin
  ptr:= nil;
  readln(ch);
  while ch⟨⟩'?' do
  begin
    searchandinsert(ptr,ch);
    readln(ch)
  end
end;
```

2.17   Sentinal nodes

In the general node insertion algorithm (Section 2.13) we saw how three special cases needed to be considered; i.e.

1. Inserting the new node as the new head node
2. Inserting the new node as the new end node
3. Inserting the new node within the body of the list

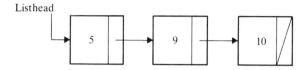

Figure 2.12   A linked list without sentinal nodes

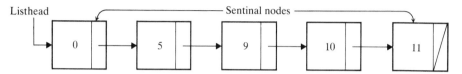

Figure 2.13   A linked list incorporating sentinal nodes

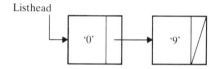

Figure 2.14   A possible empty list representation using sentinal nodes

By the introduction of dummy or *sentinal nodes* we can assure that only case 2 need be considered, thus simplifying the search-and-insert algorithm. Given a list as shown in Fig. 2.12 we can add sentinal nodes at the beginning and end of the list, creating the list shown in Fig. 2.13.

Providing the value of the data in the sentinal nodes is outside all possible data values that may be used, we need never consider the new head or new end node cases. Using this method the empty list could be indicated by a nil pointer or by a list consisting of the two sentinal nodes; e.g. if we wished to build a list of characters within the range '1'$\langle = x \langle$ = '8', the list could be initialized as shown in Fig. 2.14.

The amended procedures needed to build an ordered list using the sentinal nodes method are now given:

```
procedure BUILDORDEREDLISTWITHSENTINALS(var ptr:link);
begin
  new(ptr);
  new(endptr);
  ptr↑.data:= '0';
  ptr↑.next:= endptr;
  endptr↑.data:= '9';
  endptr↑.next:= nil;
  readln(ch);
  while ch ⟨⟩'?' do
```

```
    begin
      SENTINALSEARCHANDINSERT(ptr,ch);
      readln(ch)
    end
end;

procedure SENTINALSEARCHANDINSERT(var ptr:link;item:char);
var temp,search:link;
    inserted:boolean;
begin
    new(temp);
    temp↑.data:= item;
    temp↑.next:= nil;
    search:= ptr;
    inserted:= false;
    repeat
      if(item⟩ = search↑.data)and(item⟨ = search↑.next↑.data)then
      begin
        temp↑.next:= search↑.next;
        search↑.next:= temp;
        inserted:= true
      end
      else
        search:= search↑.next
    until inserted
end;
```

The search-and-delete procedure can be amended to make use of sentinal nodes in the following way. By assigning the value of the search item to the end sentinal node it is bound to be found. However, if it is found in the sentinal node, it is obviously not in the list proper and cannot be deleted; if it is found elsewhere, it is deleted as normal for a node within the body of the list, thus avoiding the special case of deleting the head node. The foregoing is just a simple illustration of the concept of sentinal nodes in list processing and it is left to the reader to pursue their possible uses in other more complex data structures.

2.18   Program 3

This is a menu driven program using all of the procedures defined so far and allowing the following list of activities to be carried out:

1. Build an ordered list, again with the same constraints as imposed in Programs 1 and 2.
2. Write out the contents of the list.

3. Delete a node from the list.
4. Insert a node into the list.
5. Search the list for a given node.

After execution of any section you can exit the program or return to the program menu.

2.19   Problem set 1

1. A circularly linked list is a list in which the link field of the end node contains a pointer to the head node. One of the advantages of a circular linked list is that when searching the list for more than one item the search can continue after each item is found (or not found) without having to return to the head of the list:

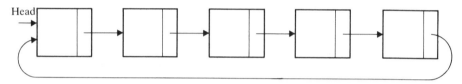

A circularly linked list

   Write the following procedures and test them in a program:
   (a) A procedure to construct a circular linked list so that the input order of data items is maintained, i.e. the first data item is assigned to the head node, the second data item is assigned to the second node, and so on.
   (b) A procedure to count the number of nodes in such a list.
   (c) A procedure to write out the data contents of each node.
   (d) A procedure to search a circular linked list for a given number of data items and to report which of the data items are in the list.

2. A doubly linked list is a list in which each node contains a pointer to both its successor and its predecessor nodes, except for the head and end nodes. This type of linking makes for easier processing of the list in certain situations:

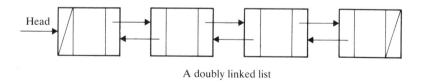

A doubly linked list

   Write the following procedures and test them in a program:
   (a) A procedure to construct an ordered doubly linked list in which each node contains as data a positive integer.

(b) A procedure to search for the first occurrence of a node containing a given data item and then to delete the node positioned two nodes earlier in the list:

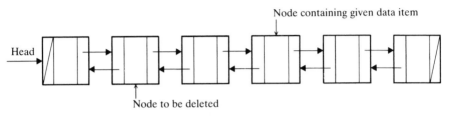

Relative position of node to be deleted

If the node to be deleted is the head node or does not exist, your procedure should take care of these special situations.

3. Write a program that traverses a singly linked list from the head node to the end node and then back to the head node, thus writing out the data items contained in the list in forward order and then in reverse order.

One method for doing this is to design a procedure that, as it traverses the list, not only writes out the data item contained in each node but also reverses each link as it proceeds. Thus two successive calls on this procedure will perform the above task yet leave the list in its original form:

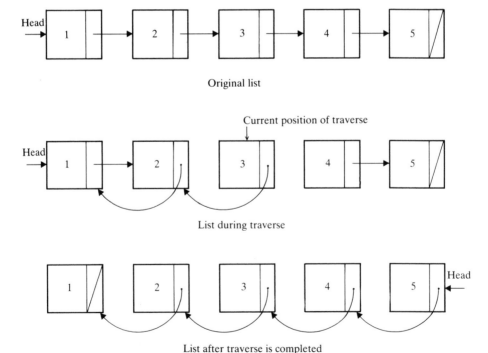

Original list

List during traverse

List after traverse is completed

4. Given two ordered singly linked lists write a procedure that will merge these two lists into a third ordered singly linked list. For example, given L1 and L2 as shown:

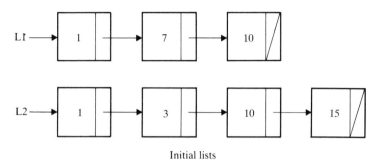

Initial lists

then the result of merging these lists is:

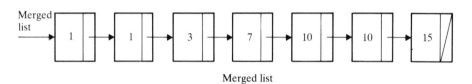

Merged list

3
Some applications of linked lists

We can make use of linked lists to model many different types of data structures and we now examine two of these.

3.1 The queue

In the earlier descriptions of linked lists we allowed insertions and deletions to occur at any point in the list. If we restrict insertions to one end of the list and deletions to the opposite end then we have a model of a *queue*.

Thus, to join an element to a queue a new end-of-list node is created and to delete an element from a queue the current head node is deleted. To see if a queue is empty it is necessary to examine the head pointer for a nil value or to examine the queue length.

3.2 The barbers' shop. A simple example of modelling a queue

A barbers shop employs one hairdresser to service customer needs. Customers are of two types:

1. those whose hairdressing needs require the hairdresser for nine minutes, we refer to these types as type A customers, and
2. those whose hairdressing needs require the hairdresser for fifteen minutes, we refer to these as type B customers.

Customers of either type arrive at random intervals of time and at the rate of five per hour. If necessary they sit in a queue awaiting their turn. We wish to simulate an eight hour period (non-stop) of activities in the shop and during this period observe the dynamics of the queue. From this observation we can see whether the barber is overworked or spending long periods in idleness.

We employ a 'time-slice' approach. This means that at fixed time intervals we test to see if any action has taken place in the shop, i.e. the barber starts work on a customer, a customer arrives and joins the queue or a customer is finished and leaves the shop, etc. Having made these observations we update the situation by any necessary amendments to the variables in our model. These activities are repeated for consecutive time slices until the complete time period of eight hours has elapsed.

3.3   Algorithm 12. A simple queue simulation

```
barbershop
begin
    set a clock to zero time
    choose a short interval of time (say 1 minute)
    repeat
        increment clock by the chosen time period
        if anything has changed since the last observation
            then update the system variables
        print queue length every 30 minutes
    until clock reaches eight hours
end
```

The probability of a customer arriving in a time period of one minute is given by

$$5 \text{ customers per hour} \,/\, 60 \text{ minutes}$$

We simulate these customer arrivals by choosing a random number between 0 and 1. If this number is less than 5/60 we say a customer arrives to join the queue; otherwise no customer arrives.

If the barber is free then a customer leaves the queue to be serviced (if the queue is empty then the barber remains idle). The type of customer being serviced determines the next time the barber will be free. Any customers arriving before that time simply join the queue. We implement Algorithm 12 as follows.

We first define the type of customer, which is used to form a linked list representing the queue of customers.

```
type link = ↑customer;
     customer = record
                    ctype:char;
                    next:link
                end;
procedure BARBERSHOP;
begin
    clock := 0;
    barberfree := 0;
    queuehead := nil;
    endqueue := nil;
    queuelength := 0;
```

```
repeat
    clock := clock + 1;
    if RANDOM < 5/60 then JOINQUEUE;
    if(clock>barberfree)and(queuelength<>0)then SERVICECUSTOMER;
    if clock mod 30 = 0 then writeln(queuelength)
until clock = 480
end;
```

Pascal does not provide a random number generator as a standard system function and therefore the following function is defined. This is a simple random number generator which only requires a seed or starting number (< 4095) assigned to the global variable rn. Once rn is assigned the function will continue to generate sequences of random numbers.

```
function RANDOM:real;
begin
    RANDOM := (rn + 1)/4096;
    rn := (125 * rn + 1)mod 4096
end;
```

The only other new procedures we need to define are those dealing with joining the queue and customers being serviced.

3.4   Algorithm 13. Joining a queue

```
joinqueue
begin
    choose type of customer at random
    if the queue is empty then create a new head
        otherwise create a new end
    increment length of queue
end
```

3.5   Algorithm 14. Servicing a customer

```
servicecustomer
begin
    set service time with respect to customer type
    set next time barber is free
    remove customer from queue and decrement queue length
end
```

Algorithms 13 and 14 are implemented as follows:

```
procedure JOINQUEUE;
begin
  new(temp);
  if RANDOM < 0.5 then temp↑.ctype:= 'A'
                  else temp↑.ctype:= 'B';
  if queuehead = nil then
  begin
    temp↑.next:= nil;
    queuehead:= temp;
    endqueue:= temp
  end
  else
  begin
    endqueue↑.next:= temp;
    temp↑.next:= nil;
    endqueue:= temp
  end;
  queuelength:= queuelength + 1
end;

procedure SERVICECUSTOMER;
begin
  if queuehead↑.ctype = 'A' then servicetime:= 9
                            else servicetime:= 15;
  barberfree:= clock + servicetime;
  temp:= queuehead;
  queuehead:= queuehead↑.next;
  dispose(temp);
  queuelength:= queuelength - 1
end;
```

3.6   Program 4

This program requires no input (other than the seed for the random number generator). When executed, the program simulates an eight hour period in a barber's shop and outputs the state of the queue at 30 minute intervals (see Figs 3.1 and 3.2).

Can we draw any conclusions from the simulator outputs? From the first output it would appear that the barber is very much overworked. The second output gives a different picture. To get a more realistic interpretation we need to run the simulator program many times and then average the queuelengths. An interesting exercise would be to amend the program as listed in Section 3.3 so that the rate of arrivals is a variable quantity and/or a bias is given to show more customers arriving around midday. The original program assumes that the probability of customers arriving is the same whatever the time of day.

Clock	Queue
30	🧍🧍🧍🧍
60	🧍🧍🧍
90	🧍🧍🧍🧍
120	🧍🧍🧍🧍🧍
150	🧍🧍🧍🧍
180	🧍🧍🧍🧍🧍🧍
210	🧍🧍🧍
240	🧍🧍🧍🧍🧍🧍🧍
270	🧍🧍🧍🧍🧍🧍
300	🧍🧍🧍🧍🧍🧍🧍
330	🧍🧍🧍🧍🧍🧍🧍
360	🧍🧍🧍🧍🧍🧍🧍
390	🧍🧍🧍🧍🧍🧍🧍
420	🧍🧍🧍🧍🧍🧍
450	🧍🧍🧍🧍🧍🧍
480	🧍🧍🧍🧍🧍🧍

Queuelength at 30 minute intervals

Figure 3.1   Simulator output 1

3.7   The stack

If we restrict insertions and deletions to only occur at one end of a list, the head, then we model a very important and useful data structure called a *stack*. Stacks are sometimes referred to as push-down lists or first-in-last-out lists. Suppose that two stack operators *PUSH* and *POP* exist such that PUSH is an operator that takes an operand and pushes (inserts) it as the top element of a stack and POP is an operator that pops (deletes) the top element of a stack. Figure 3.3 shows the history of a stack during repeated applications of PUSH and POP.

The following procedures execute the PUSH and POP operations for a stack whose elements consist of simple nodes defined as follows:

```
type link = ↑node;
     node = record
                data:integer;
                next:link
            end;
```

Clock	Queue
30	Queue empty, barber is idle
60	🧍
90	Queue empty, barber is idle
120	🧍🧍
150	Queue empty, barber is idle
180	Queue empty, barber is idle
210	Queue empty, barber is idle
240	Queue empty, barber is idle
270	Queue empty, barber is idle
300	Queue empty, barber is idle
330	Queue empty, barber is idle
360	🧍
390	🧍🧍
420	Queue empty, barber is idle
450	🧍
480	Queue empty, barber is idle

Queuelength at 30 minute intervals

Figure 3.2   Simulator output 2

The top element in the stack is pointed to by a variable of type link and called *stackheadptr*. If at any time the value of this pointer is NIL, the stack is empty. When popping items this pointer must always be tested as any attempt to pop an item from an empty stack will cause an error. Also, if the stack size is limited, a check must be made to ensure stack overflow does not occur.

```
procedure PUSH(var ptr:link;item:integer);
var temp:link;
begin
   new(temp);
   temp↑.data:= item;
   temp↑.next:= ptr;
   ptr:= temp
end;
```

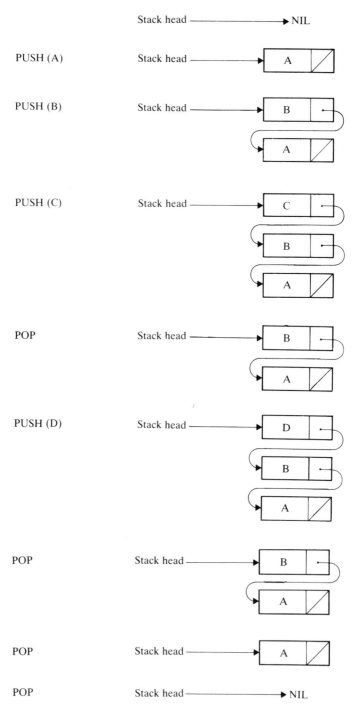

Figure 3.3 Stack history during the execution of a PUSH–POP sequence

```
procedure POP(var ptr:link;var item:integer);
var temp:link;
begin
  if ptr<>nil then
  begin
    item := ptr↑.data;
    temp := ptr;
    ptr := ptr↑.next;
    dispose(temp)
  end
end;
```

3.8   Using a stack to change number bases

Changing a number from base ten to an equivalent number in any other base
($1 <$ base < 10) can be accomplished by repeated division of the number by the
new base, until a zero result is obtained, saving the remainder after each division
and then writing out the remainders in reverse order. This process is illustrated
by the following example.

Change the denary number 27 to an equivalent number in base 4:

First division: 4) 27
                             6   remainder 3
Second division: 4) 6
                             1   remainder 2
Third division: 4) 1
                             0   remainder 1

After the third division the result is zero and therefore the remainders are written
out in their reverse order, giving the following result:

$$27_{10} \equiv 123_4$$

The first remainder is the last to be written out while the last remainder is the
first to be written out. We can model this last-in-first-out situation very
conveniently by means of a stack.

3.9   Algorithm 15.   The number base problem

```
changenumberbase
begin
set stack to be empty
  repeat
    divide denary number by new base
    push value of remainder to a stack
    replace denary number by result of division
  until result of division is zero
end
```

If a stack is represented by a linked list then pushing an item to a stack is the same as creating a new head and popping an item is equivalent to deleting the head. Algorithm 15 is implemented as follows:

```
procedure CHANGENUMBERBASE;
var item:integer;
begin
  stackheadptr:= nil;
  read(number,base); {number > 0}
  while number <> 0 do
  begin
    item:= number mod base;
    PUSH(stackheadptr,item);
    number:= number div base
  end;
  PRINTSTACK(stackheadptr);
  writeln
end;
```

The only new procedure used is PRINTSTACK, which prints out the contents of the stack:

```
procedure PRINTSTACK(ptr:link);
begin
  while ptr<>nil do
  begin
    write(ptr↑.data);
    ptr:= ptr↑.next
  end
end;
```

3.10   Program 5

When executed the program prompts the user to input a denary number (> 0) and the value of the new base. The program will print out the equivalent number value in this new base.

3.11   An application of stacks to the evaluation of arithmetic expressions

Before proceeding to investigate the evaluation of arithmetic expressions we first of all specify what we mean by an arithmetic expression. For the purpose of this exercise we consider the vocabulary of arithmetic expressions to consist of the positive integers, the binary operators $+, *, /$ and $-$ and matching parentheses. Expressions are constructed according to the following rules:

1. A positive integer is an expression.

2. If $\#$ is a binary operator and E1 and E2 are expressions then E1 $\#$ E2 is an expression.
3. If E is an expression then (E) is also an expression.

Thus we can see that

> 6   is an expression by rule 1,
> 6 + 7   is an expression by rules 1 and 2,
> 6 * (7 + 4)   is an expression by rules 1, 2 and 3.

Expressions are evaluated using *left grouping* and *operator precedence*. From schooldays we remember that the operators $*$ and $/$ are 'stronger' and therefore take precedence over the operators $+$ and $-$. Furthermore, this precedence can be altered by the use of parentheses.

Taking as an example the expression $12 * (5 + 6)$ we can see that without the parentheses the subexpression $12 * 5$ is evaluated first, giving a final result of 66. However, the presence of the parentheses causes the subexpression of $5 + 6$ to be evaluated first, giving a final result of 132.

If an expression contains operators of equal strengths then it is evaluated using left grouping. The expression $12 + 6 - 3 + 2$ is evaluated by left grouping as indicated by its fully parenthesized form given below:

$$(((12 + 6) - 3) + 2)$$

Any expressions of the type just described can be evaluated by the use of two stacks, one stack to hold operators and a second stack to hold operands. The following evaluation algorithm maintains the left-to-right grouping and the rules of operator precedence. The symbols of the expression are read from left to right. (Note that parentheses are considered to be members of the class of operators and have the lowest precedence.)

3.12   Algorithm 16. Stack evaluation

```
stackevaluation
begin
    set operand and operator stacks empty
    get first symbol of expression
    while expression is not exhausted do
        begin
            if symbol is an operand then PUSH to operand stack
            else
            if symbol is a left parenthesis then PUSH to operator stack
            else
            if symbol is a right parenthesis then
            begin
                POP operator stack
                while popped operator not a left parenthesis do
```

```
        begin
          apply operator to top two operands on
            operand stack, POP these two elements
            and PUSH result to operand stack
          POP operator stack
        end
      end
      else
      if operator stack is empty then push symbol to operator stack
      else
      begin
        while top element of operator stack is
            stronger than symbol do
        begin
          POP operator stack
          apply popped operator to top two elements
            of operand stack, POP these two elements
            and PUSH result to operand stack
        end
        else
        PUSH symbol to operator stack
      get next symbol of expression
    end
    while operator stack not empty do
    begin
      POP operator stack
      apply popped operator to top two elements
        of operand stack, POP these two elements
        and PUSH result to operand stack
    end
end
```

We now apply Algorithm 16 to the following expression:

$$3*(5-3)$$

As each input symbol is read the action is noted and the stack history shown (see Fig. 3.4). Termination of the expression is signalled by a full stop.

3.13   Program 6

This program implements Algorithm 16. The user is prompted to input an arithmetic expression. The program assumes that the expression is correctly formed according to the rules given at the beginning of Section 3.11.

3.14   Using linked lists for the storage of sparse arrays

In many real-life computing problems, i.e. structural design, solution of differential equations, etc., it is often necessary to deal with large arrays in which many

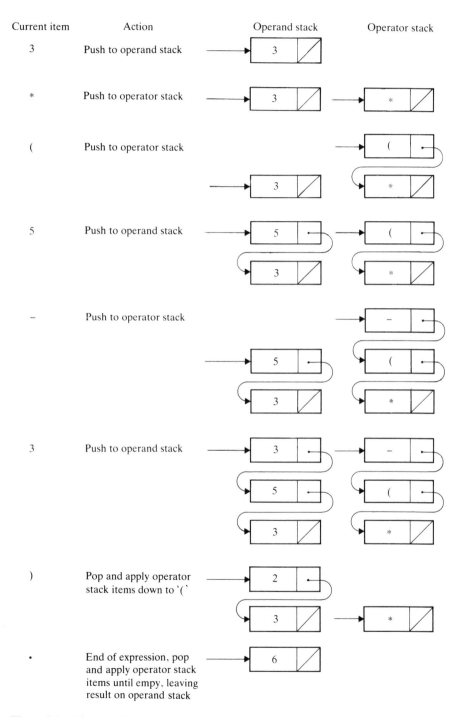

Figure 3.4 History of the operator and operand stacks during evaluation of the expression $3*(5-3)$

0	0	3.5	0	0	0	0	0
0	1.2	0	0	0	0	0	0
0	0	0	0	0	0	0	0
0	0	0	0	0	0	0	5.5
0	0	0	0	2.5	0	0	0
0	0	0	0	0	0	6.7	0

Figure 3.5   A typical sparse matrix representation

of the elements have a zero value. Such arrays with about 10 per cent non-zero elements are called *sparse arrays*. By large we infer arrays of the order 1000 by 1000 and very few computers can provide the necessary storage for 1 000 000 elements. However, if, as mentioned, many of the elements in these arrays are zero, it is well worth investigating some alternative methods of storage to those outlined in Section 1.2. Consider the two-dimensional sparse array shown in Fig. 3.5.

We can see that only 5 out of the 48 elements are non-zero and for all practical purposes these are the only elements that need to be stored. A simple method to do this is to use a 3-tuple for each element such that each 3-tuple consists of a row index, a column index and a value. Hence for the sparse array given, the following list of 3-tuples would suffice:

$$1,3,3.5$$
$$2,2,1.2$$
$$4,8,5.5$$
$$5,5,2.5$$
$$6,7,6.7$$

These 3-tuples can be stored in row order as a conventional array (see Fig. 3.6); thus, if a two-dimensional sparse array has N non-zero elements, a one-dimensional array of size $3 * N$ is required for storage purposes.

As a storage system for sparse arrays this method leaves a lot to be desired as most sparse arrays represent items in matrix manipulations and therefore often

| 1 | 3 | 3.5 | 2 | 2 | 1.2 | 4 | 8 | 5.5 | 5 | 5 | 2.5 | 6 | 7 | 6.7 |

Figure 3.6   Storage of sparse matrix data using a one-dimensional array

Figure 3.7   Storage of sparse matrix data using a linked list of 3-tuples

non-zero elements need to be added or deleted. If we use a storage array of size
3 * N, when elements are to be added this array is too small and when elements
are deleted then movement in the storage array of existing 3-tuples is required.
Thus again we see the limitations of a static storage system when modelling a
dynamic situation.

An obvious improvement is to include with each 3-tuple a link to the next
3-tuple and to store these as a linked list of 3-tuples instead of using an array. If
non-zero elements are to be added or deleted, we can use the insertion and
deletion algorithms given in Sections 2.13 and 2.14, thus making a much more
sensible and usable storage system. Figure 3.7 illustrates the linked list for the
sparse array given in Fig. 3.5.

This linked list can be built as an ordered list using the row indexes as the
primary ordering. If two or more row indexes are the same, the column index is
used for ordering. Although this is an improvement on the static array storage
system, it is still rather simplistic for many real-life problems. More information
will normally be stored about each non-zero element, i.e. is it the element first in
its row or column?, etc. These structures are dealt with in some detail in other
texts and are an extremely important foundation for many of the most
important business data processing applications.

3.15   Further list processing.   List builder and selector functions

THE SELECTOR FUNCTIONS

As already mentioned a list consists of a head and a tail. We now investigate
functions which return the head or tail of a list as values, thus enabling any item
in the list to be selected by the application of such functions. We are given the list
L1 whose nodes each contain an integer, as shown in Fig. 3.8.

The selector function HEAD returns the data contained in the head node of
the list; thus

HEAD(L1) returns the integer 3.

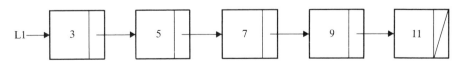

Figure 3.8   An ordered linked list of integers

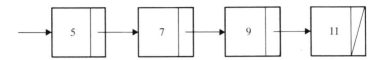

Figure 3.9   The result of applying the function TAIL to the list given in Fig. 3.8

The selector function TAIL returns a pointer to the list remaining after the head has been removed as value (the TAIL of the list):

> TAIL(L1) returns the list shown in Fig. 3.9.

Combination of the functions head and tail allows any single data item in the list to be selected. For example,

HEAD(TAIL(L1)) selects the node containing the data item 5

HEAD(TAIL(TAIL(L1))) selects the node containing the data item 7

THE CONSTRUCTOR FUNCTION

The constructor or builder function *prefix* is used to build lists as follows. When called it accepts a data item and a list as arguments. It prefixes the list with a node containing the data item and returns a pointer to the new list as value. For example,

> PREFIX(30,L1) returns a pointer to the list shown in Fig. 3.10.

It should be fairly obvious that using the function PREFIX iteratively provides yet another way of building lists. We implement these three list functions as follows:

> function HEAD(ptr:link):integer;
> begin
>   HEAD:= ptr↑.data
> end;

> function TAIL(ptr:link):link;
> begin
>   TAIL:= ptr↑.next
> end;

(Note that the functions HEAD and TAIL assume non-empty lists.)

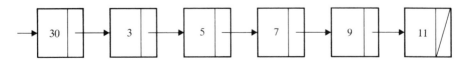

Figure 3.10   The result of applying the function PREFIX to the list given in Fig. 3.8

```
function PREFIX(item:integer;ptr:link):link;
var temp:link;
begin
  new(temp);
  temp↑.data := item;
  temp↑.next := ptr;
  PREFIX := temp
end;
```

We can now use these basic list processing functions to construct more complex list functions. We give as an example a function designed to reverse the order of the nodes in a list. The idea behind the function 'reverse' is quite simple and is outlined in the following algorithm.

3.16   Algorithm 17. Reversing the nodes in a linked list

```
function reversealist(list)
begin
  set result to be an empty list
  if list has a nil value then return an empty list
  else
  repeat
    prefix result with the head of list
    list becomes tail of list
  until list is empty
  return result
end
```

We can follow the execution of Algorithm 17 by applying it to the list given below. Snapshots of the various stages are given in Fig. 3.11. We implement Algorithm 17 by the function defined below:

```
function REVERSE(ptr:link):link;
var result:link;
begin
  result := nil;
  if ptr = nil then REVERSE := result
  else
  begin
    repeat
      result := PREFIX(HEAD(ptr),result);
      ptr := TAIL(ptr)
    until ptr = nil;
    REVERSE := result
  end
end;
```

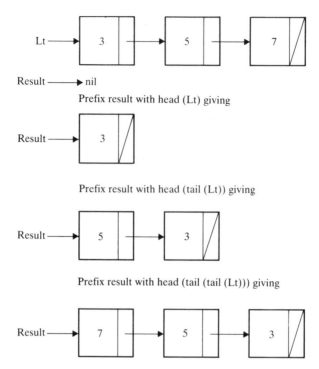

Figure 3.11   Application of list functions to reverse a list

Thus, assuming the list L1 as defined earlier, a call to reverse L1 is

$$L2 := REVERSE(L1);$$

3.17   Using linked lists to represent sets of objects

An interesting application of lists and list functions is to be seen in using lists to represent sets of objects. Given the set of integers $S1 = \{1,2,3,4\}$ we can easily build a list using the prefix function to represent this set (see Fig. 3.12).

We now turn our attention to designing list functions that define operations on ordered sets. By ordered sets we mean that there exists an order relation between the elements of a set; in each of the following examples we make use of the implied order relation between positive integers.

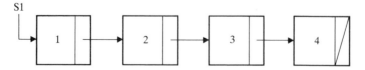

Figure 3.12   The ordered set $\{1, 2, 3, 4\}$ represented by a list

3.18   Set intersection

Given the sets S1 and S2 we define the *intersection* of these sets (shown in the Venn diagram and written S1 ∩ S2) as being the set containing those elements that belong to both S1 and S2 (Fig. 3.13). For example,

$$\text{if } S1 = \{1,3,5,7\}$$
$$\text{and } S2 = \{3,7,11\}$$
$$\text{then } S1 \cap S2 = \{3,7\}$$

If we represent S1 and S2 as linked lists, we approach the problem of defining a function to perform the operation of intersection, as illustrated by Algorithm 18.

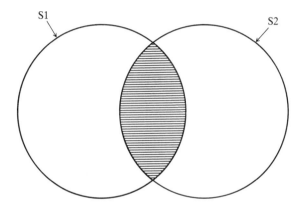

Figure 3.13   Venn diagram showing the intersection of two sets

3.19   Algorithm 18.   Intersection of two ordered sets

```
function intersection (S1,S2)
begin
    initialize result set to empty
    if S1 and S2 are empty then return result set
    else
    repeat
        if head(S1) = head(S2)then assign head(S1) to
            result set and delete head(S1) and head(S2)
        else
        if head(S1) < head(S2)then delete head(S1)
        else
        delete head(S2)
    until S1 or S2 is empty
    end
```

We now work through the earlier example given in order to illustrate the way Algorithm 18 works.

$\left[\begin{array}{l}\{1,3,5,7\} \text{ Heads are not equal} \\ \{3,7,11\} \text{ Head (S1) is less than head (S2). Delete head (S1)}\end{array}\right.$

$\left[\begin{array}{l}\{3,5,7\} \text{ Heads are equal. Put head (S1) into intersection set. } \{3\} \\ \{3,7,11\} \text{ Delete head (S1) and head (S2)}\end{array}\right.$

$\left[\begin{array}{l}\{5,7\} \text{ Heads are not equal} \\ \{7,11\} \text{ Head (S1) is less than head (S2). Delete head (S1)}\end{array}\right.$

$\left[\begin{array}{l}\{7\} \text{ Heads are equal. Put head (S1) into intersection set. } \{3,7\} \\ \{7,11\} \text{ Delete head (S1) and head (S2)}\end{array}\right.$

$\left[\begin{array}{l}\{\ \} \\ \{11\} \text{ S1 is empty, algorithm stops giving the set } (S1 \cap S2) = \{3,7\}\end{array}\right.$

Algorithm 18 is implemented by the following functions:

```
function INTERSECTION(ptr1,ptr2:link):link;
var result:link;
begin
  result:= nil;
  if(ptr1 = nil) or (ptr2 = nil)then INTERSECTION:= result
  else
  begin
    repeat
      if HEAD(ptr1) = HEAD(ptr2) then
      begin
        result:= PREFIX(HEAD(ptr1),result);
        ptr1:= TAIL(ptr1);
        ptr2:= TAIL(ptr2)
      end
      else
      if HEAD(ptr1) < HEAD(ptr2) then ptr1:= TAIL(ptr1)
      else
      ptr2:= TAIL(ptr2)
    until(ptr1 = nil)or(ptr2 = nil)
    INTERSECTION:= REVERSE(result)
  end
end;
```

3.20 Set union

Given the sets S1 and S2 we define the *union* of these sets (shown shaded in the Venn diagram and written S1 ∪ S2) as being the set containing those elements belonging to either S1 or S2 (Fig. 3.14). For example,

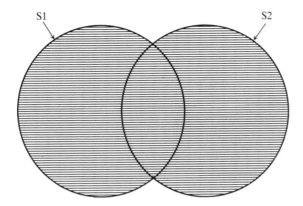

Figure 3.14   Venn diagram showing the union of two sets

$$\text{if}\quad S1 = \{1,3,5,7\}$$
$$\text{and}\quad S2 = \{3,5,7,9,10\}$$
$$\text{then } S1 \cup S2 = \{1,3,5,7,9,10\}$$

Using the list representations of S1 and S2 as given earlier, the following algorithm produces the union set.

3.21   Algorithm 19. The union of two ordered sets

```
function union(S1,S2)
begin
    initialize the result set to empty
    if S1 and S2 are empty return the result set
    else
    repeat
        if S1 is empty and S2 is not empty then assign head(S2) to result set
            and delete head(S2)
        else
        if S2 is empty and S1 is not empty then assign head(S1) to result set
            and delete head(S1)
        else
        if head(S1) = head(S2)then assign head(S1) to
            result set and delete head(S1) and head(S2)
        else
        if head(S1) < head(S2)then assign head(S1) to
            result set and delete head(S1)
        else
        assign head(S2) to result set and delete head(S2)
    until S1 and S2 are empty
end
```

As we did for intersection, we now illustrate the working of Algorithm 19 by the following example:

$$S1 = \{2,3\} \text{ and } S2 = \{3,4\}$$

$\left[\begin{array}{l} \{2,3\} \text{ Head(S1) is less than head(S2). Put head(S1) into union set } \{2\} \\ \{3,4\} \text{ Delete head(S1).} \end{array}\right.$

$\left[\begin{array}{l} \{3\} \text{ Head(S1) = head(S2). Put head(S1) into union set. } \{2,3\} \\ \{3,4\} \text{ Delete head(S1) and head(S2)} \end{array}\right.$

$\left[\begin{array}{l} \{\ \} \text{ S1 is empty. Put head(S2) into union set. } \{2,3,4\} \\ \{4\} \text{ Delete head(S2)} \end{array}\right.$

$\left[\begin{array}{l} \{\ \} \\ \{\ \} \text{ Both sets are empty, algorithm stops giving the set (S1 } \cup \text{ S2) = } \{2,3,4\} \end{array}\right.$

Algorithm 19 is implemented as follows:

```
function UNION(ptr1,ptr2:link):link;
var result:link;
begin
  result:= nil;
  if(ptr1 = nil)and(ptr2 = nil)then UNION:= result
  else
  begin
    repeat
    if(ptr2 = nil)and(ptr1<>nil)then
    begin
      result:= PREFIX(HEAD(ptr1),result);
      ptr1:= TAIL(ptr1)
    end
    else
    if(ptr2<>nil)and(ptr1 = nil)then
    begin
      result:= PREFIX(HEAD(ptr2),result);
      ptr2:= TAIL(ptr2)
    end
    else
    if HEAD(ptr1) < HEAD(ptr2)then
    begin
      result:= PREFIX(HEAD(ptr1),result);
      ptr1:= TAIL(ptr1)
    end
    else
    if HEAD(ptr1) = HEAD(ptr2)then
    begin
```

```
          result := PREFIX(HEAD(ptr1),result);
          ptr1 := TAIL(ptr1);
          ptr2 := TAIL(ptr2)
        end
        else
        begin
          result := PREFIX(HEAD(ptr2),result);
          ptr2 := TAIL(ptr2)
          end
        until(ptr1 = nil)and(ptr2 = nil);
      UNION := REVERSE(result)
      end
    end;
```

3.22 Membership of a set

Given a set S1 and an item i the set function $i \in S1$ tests to see if i belongs to, or is
an element of, the set S1. Implementing this function is simply a matter of
amending one of the list searching procedures previously defined. We choose a
non-recursive version:

```
    function ISANELEMENTOF(ptr:link;item:integer):boolean;
    var found:boolean;
    begin
      found := false;
      if ptr = nil then writeln('Set is empty')
      else
      repeat
        if item = HEAD(ptr)then found := true
        else
        ptr := TAIL(ptr)
        until found or(ptr = nil);
    ISANELEMENTOF := found
    end;
```

3.23 Equality of two ordered sets

To test if two ordered sets are equal we can compare the heads of each list
representing the sets and if they are the same we can replace both lists by their
tails and again compare their heads. If at any time the heads are not equal or
either list becomes empty before the other, we know that the lists do not
represent equal sets:

```
        function EQUALSETS(ptr1,ptr2:link):boolean;
        var listend,equal:boolean;
```

```
begin
  listend := false;
  equal := true;
  repeat
    if(ptr1 = nil)and(ptr2 = nil)then listend := true
    else
    if(ptr1 = nil)or(ptr2 = nil)then
    begin
      equal := false;
      listend := true
    end
    else
    if HEAD(ptr1)< >HEAD(ptr2)then
    begin
      equal := false;
      listend := true
    end
    else
    begin
      ptr1 := TAIL(ptr1);
      ptr2 := TAIL(ptr2)
    end
  until listend;
  EQUALSETS := equal
end;
```

3.24   Set inclusion

Again given the sets S1 and S2 and if S2 contains S1 we say that S1 is a *subset* of S2 (written S1 ⊂ S2). It is fairly obvious from the Venn diagram that if the inter-

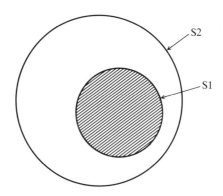

Figure 3.15   Venn diagram showing set inclusion

section of S1 and S2 gives a set which is equal to S1 then S1 is a subset of S2 (Fig. 3.15).

```
function SUBSET(ptr1,ptr2:link):boolean;
begin
  if EQUALSETS(INTERSECTION(ptr1,ptr2),ptr1)then
  SUBSET:= true
  else
  SUBSET:= false
end;
```

3.25   Set difference

Our final set operation is one that is designed to return the *difference* set of two ordered sets. The difference between the two sets S1 and S2 (written S1 − S2) is defined as the set containing those elements of S1 that are not elements of S2,

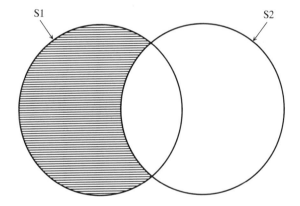

Figure 3.16   Venn diagram showing the difference of two sets

and again this is illustrated by the shaded area in the Venn diagram (Fig. 3.16). For example,

$$\text{if } S1 = \{1,2\}$$
$$\text{and } S2 = \{2,3\}$$
$$\text{then } S1 - S2 = \{1\}$$

3.26   Algorithm 20.   The difference of two ordered sets

```
function difference(S1,S2)
begin
  initialize result set to empty
if S1 is empty then return result set
  else
```

```
if S2 is empty then return S1
else
repeat
  if head(S1) = head(S2) then delete head(S1) and head(S2)
  else
  if head(S1)< head(S2)then assign head(S1)to result
    set and delete head(S1)
  else delete head(S2)
  until S1 or S2 is empty
end
```

Algorithm 20 is implemented by the following function:

```
function DIFFERENCE(ptr1,ptr2:link):link;
var result:link;
begin
  result:= nil;
  if ptr1 = nil then DIFFERENCE:= result
  else
  if ptr2 = nil then DIFFERENCE:= ptr1
  else
  begin
    repeat
      if HEAD(ptr1) = HEAD(ptr2)then
      begin
        ptr1:= TAIL(ptr1);
        ptr2:= TAIL(ptr2)
      end
      else
      if HEAD(ptr1)< HEAD(ptr2)then
      begin
        result:= PREFIX(HEAD(ptr1),result);
        ptr1:= TAIL(ptr1)
      end
      else
      ptr2:= TAIL(ptr2)
    until (ptr1 = nil)or(ptr2 = nil);
    DIFFERENCE:= REVERSE(result)
  end
end;
```

3.27   Program 7

This program illustrates the use of lists and list functions applied to the subject
of sets and set operations. The user is prompted to input data (in this case,

positive integers terminated by any negative integer) to construct two ordered sets. The program then outputs the result of each of the set operations described in this section. To illustrate the test for set membership the user is prompted to input a suitable element. This test is carried out only on one of the sets, this being considered enough demonstration. For clarity the program only deals with non-empty sets.

3.28 Complex list structures

Up to now we have been concerned with representations of simple lists and ordered lists. We now examine a more abstract definition of ordered lists.

An ordered list is either empty or contains elements:

$$x_1, x_2, x_3, \ldots, x_n$$

where the elements are called *atoms* and are elements of some set of objects S ($x_2 \in S$). Examples of possible sets S are:

1. The days of the week
2. The months of the year
3. The letters of an alphabet

The non-empty ordered list L1 is written as follows:

$$L1 = (a, b, c, d)$$

while the empty list L2 is written

$$L2 = (\,)$$

We have already seen that such lists can be conveniently represented by a linked data structure. If we now allow the elements of a list to be either atoms or lists then we have a *generalized* list. Some examples of generalized lists are now given:

1. $$L3 = (a, (b, c)\,)$$

L3 is a list with two elements: the first element is the atom 'a' and the second element is the list (b, c). We can picture this list as follows:

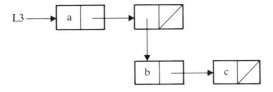

2. $$L4 = (a, (\,), b\,)$$

L4 is a list with three elements: the first element is the atom 'a', the second is an empty list and the third element is the atom 'b'. Again we can picture the list as follows:

Using the notion of a generalized list we can design quite large complex list structures. For example, given the list expression:

$$L5 = (\ (c, (e), d),\ a,\ (f,\ (h,\ i),\ g),b,\ c)$$

the resulting list structure is given in Fig. 3.17.

To represent generalized lists by linked data structures we can use nodes that are modelled by variant records (Fig. 3.18).

The tag field is set to true if the data/sublist field contains a pointer to a list. If the data/sublist field contains an atom then the tag field is set to false.

Such a node is defined in Pascal as follows:

```
type link = ^node;
     node = record
                next:link;
                case tag:boolean of
                false:(data:char);
                true :(sublist:link)
            end;
```

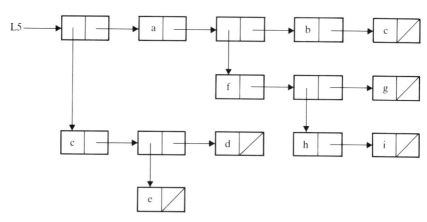

Figure 3.17   A generalized list structure

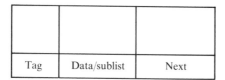

Figure 3.18   A variant record representing a node in a generalized list structure

We now examine the use of a complex data structure as opposed to a complex list structure as a solution to the following problem.

3.29   The library problem

A dynamic data structure is to be used to store information about the stock of a small library. The information stored is to include author names and book titles, both being kept in alphabetical order. Facilities are to be available that enable the following operations to be carried out on the stored data structure:

1. The addition of new authors and book titles
2. The deletion of authors from the author list, including all books attributed to them
3. The addition of new book titles to existing authors
4. The deletion of individual books by a given author
5. The printing of all information in the library data structure
6. The printing of all book titles by a given author

To build a data structure suitable for the above we use two types of nodes. For the linked list of authors we use nodes with four fields as shown in Fig. 3.19 and

Field 1 Author name	Field 2 Pointer to end of booklist	Field 3 Pointer to head of booklist	Field 4 Link to next author

Figure 3.19   An author node

Field 1 Book title	Field 2 Link to next book title

Figure 3.20   A book node

for the linked lists of books we use nodes with only two fields (see Fig. 3.20). The general pattern of the complex data structure used for the library problem is given by Fig. 3.21.

The procedures needed to implement a solution to the library problem as outlined are very similar to those already detailed and defined in previous problems. Therefore, instead of listing these procedures a structure diagram is given (see Fig. 3.22), which together with the program listing in Section 3.3 is felt

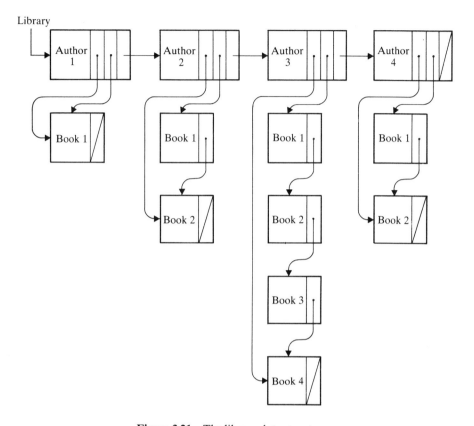

Figure 3.21   The library data structure

gives enough information for the reader to understand this particular solution to the problem.

While the program enables all the stated tasks to be carried out no provision is made for writing out the information held in the data structure to a tape or disk file. This is left as a task for the reader to do.

3.30   Program 8

The program is menu based and illustrates the use of dynamic variables matching the dynamic nature of the problem.

3.31   Problem set 2

1. The following Pascal recursive procedure reads characters until a full stop is encountered and then writes out the list of characters read, in reverse order.

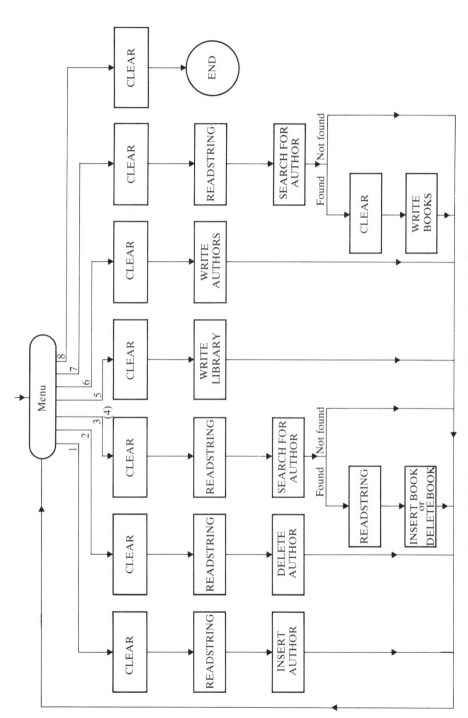

Figure 3.22 Program structure used in a solution to the library problem

This procedure is possible because of the availability of local variables.

```
procedure REVERSE;
var ch:char;
begin
  read(ch);
  if ch ⟨ ⟩ '.' then REVERSE;
  write(ch)
end;
```

It works as follows: each time the procedure is called, space is allocated on a stack for the local variable 'ch'. Once the full stop is read, each procedure call is completed by writing out the contents of the stack of local variables. The allocation and stacking of local variables is taken care of by the language implementation and therefore does not normally concern the programmer; however, assuming that only global variables are available write a program that will implement this procedure.

2. Two sparse arrays are represented in memory by linked lists of triples. Each triple contains a data item together with its row and column index. Write and test a procedure that will add two such array representations together. Note that, given two matrices each M by N, matrix addition is carried out on an elementwise basis as indicated in the following diagram:

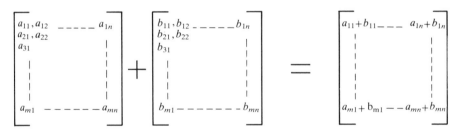

Matrix addition

3. The barbershop simulation program (Program 4) can be amended so that the barber is represented by a Pascal record as shown:

idle	
busy	
nextfree	

The idle field keeps a running total of the barber's idle time and the busy field contains a boolean that records the fact of whether the barber is busy or not at any given instant of time. Thus, given the following declarations:

```
type link = ^person;
     person = record
                    servicetime:integer;
                    next:link
              end;
     person2 = record
                     idle,nextfree:integer;
                     busy:boolean
                end;
var . .
      . .
     barber:person2;
```

an outline of the main procedure becomes

```
procedure BARBERSHOP;
begin
  clock := 0;
  with barber do
  begin
    idle := 0;
    busy := false;
    nextfree := 0
  end;
  queuehead := nil; endqueue := nil; queuelength := 0; clock := 0;
  repeat
    clock := clock + 1;
    if RANDOM < 5/60 then JOINQUEUE;
    . . .
    . . . etc.
    if not barber.busy then barber.idle := barber.idle + 1
  until clock := 480
end;
```

Rewrite the barbershop program using these ideas and include in the program a printout of the following information for each minute of a 30 minute simulation period:

> Time shown by clock
> Length of queue
> Total idle time
> Whether the barber is busy or not
> At what time he will be next free

4. A small supermarket has three checkout points. Customers arrive at these checkouts at the rate of 40 per hour. The time taken for each customer to have their purchases checked and paid for varies (randomly) between three

and eight minutes. Using the concept of a Pascal record to represent each checkout simulate a continuous eight hour period at the checkouts. (Note that customers arriving at the checkouts always join the smallest queue. If queues are of equal length then customers join the first available queue in strict order.)

The necessary data structures can be pictured as shown in the diagram below. The program should output information about each checkout at fixed periods of time using the following format:

Clock = 30   Checkout ONE   Checkout TWO   Checkout THREE
              queuelength = 1   queuelength = 0   queuelength = 0
              idle   = 3   idle   = 10   idle   = 20
              busy   = TRUE   busy   = TRUE   busy   = FALSE
              nextfree   = 32   nextfree   = 31   nextfree   = 25

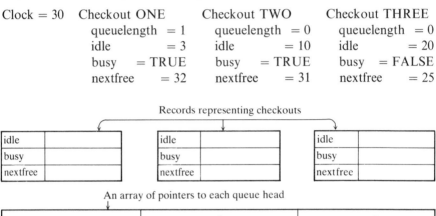

Records representing checkouts

An array of pointers to each queue head

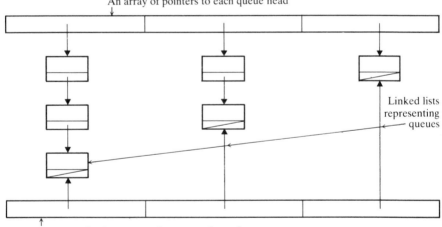

Linked lists representing queues

An array of pointers to each queue end

Suggested data structures

5. A robot lives on an infinite flat plane. The plane is divided into squares which form a grid. The robot can move in the direction it is facing along the grid lines. When it arrives at the intersection of a pair of grid lines it can take one of four possible actions:

Go straight ahead
Turn right

Turnleft
Turnaround (change direction by 180 degrees)

The robot starting at any point on the grid takes a random walk; i.e. at each grid line intersection it executes at random one of the four choices given above. The following diagram illustrates a random walk:

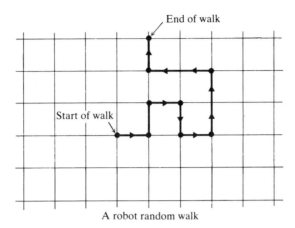

A robot random walk

Write a program, that not only simulates such a random walk but also prints out the instructions in order that the robot can return to its starting point.

For example, the instructions for the return journey of the walk given in the diagram are:

Turnaround
Straightahead
Turnleft
Straightahead
Straightahead
Turnright
Straightahead
Straightahead
Turnright
Straightahead
Turnright
Straightahead
Turnleft
Straightahead
Turnleft
Straightahead
Turnright
Straightahead
Stop

6. Imagine that a particular implementation of Pascal does not allow the creation of dynamic data structures in the usual way; i.e. no pointer variables are implemented. It is proposed to write a program that simulates dynamic data storage and allows the user to create and process singly linked lists. The store from which nodes will be obtained dynamically will be simulated by a Pascal array. Data items will be restricted to positive integers and pointers will be represented by integer array indexes.

Initially the store of nodes will appear as follows:

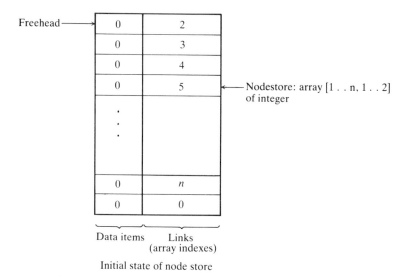

Initial state of node store

After the creation of an ordered list containing the data items

$$2, 5, 7, 10, 15, 20, 30$$

the state of the store will be changed to that shown below:

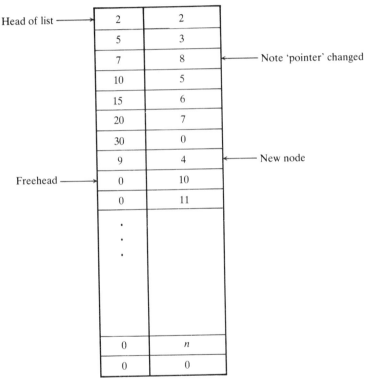

State of node store after list is created

Assuming a node containing the data item 9 is to be inserted in the list, the state of the store after insertion is

State of node store after node insertion

Two of the procedures needed will be to emulate the getting and returning of nodes from the store, analogous to the Pascal commands NEW and DISPOSE. Incorporate these ideas into a program that allows the building and processing of singly linked lists in a Pascal-like fashion.

4
Non-linear data structures

4.1 Trees

Trees are one of the most important non-linear structures used in computer science. A tree structure is one in which items of data are related by branches. A very common example is the ancestors tree (see Fig. 4.1). This tree shows the ancestors of Bill. His parents are John and Sue. John's parents are Alf and Flo who are also the grandparents of Bill on his father's side. Going back one more generation we see that Colin, Mavis, Ray and Dorothy are Bill's great grandparents.

Using the concept of a node to hold items of data, a tree structure can be defined formally as follows:

A tree is a finite set of one or more nodes, such that: there is a special node called the root and the remaining nodes are partitioned into $n > = 0$ disjoint sets, $T_1, \ldots, T_n$, where each of these sets is called a subtree of the root.

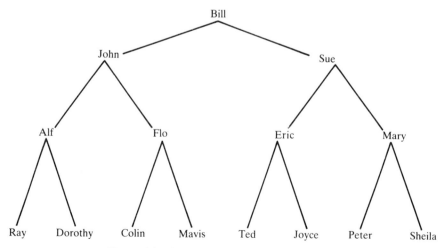

Figure 4.1 An ancestor tree showing pedigree

This is a recursive definition, defining a tree in terms of trees; thus, returning to Fig. 4.1 we can see that John and Sue are roots of the subtrees of Bill, while Alf and Flo are roots of the subtrees of John, etc. Every item of data in the tree is therefore the root of a subtree of the whole tree. In our example the great grandparent nodes are the roots of trees with no subtrees. Nodes with this property are called *leaf* or *terminal* nodes. The root node of the whole tree is Bill.

A DIFFERENT TREE RELATIONSHIP

The tree shown in Fig. 4.1 illustrates the branch relation 'is the parent of'. Thus we can see that

Ted is the parent of Eric,
Mary is the parent of Sue,
John is the parent of Bill, etc.

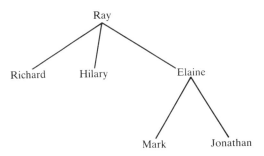

Figure 4.2 A typical family tree

We now consider the branch relation 'is the child of'. An example of such a tree is given in Fig. 4.2. From this tree we can see that

Richard is the child of Ray,
Hilary is the child of Ray,
Elaine is the child of Ray,
Mark is the child of Elaine,
Jonathan is the child of Elaine.

We can also see that Mark and Jonathan are the grandchildren of Ray.

Generally when describing trees the terminology used is based on the family tree concept given by Fig. 4.2, i.e. each node being thought of as the parent of the root nodes of its subtrees.

We now give some of the more common terms using the tree in Fig. 4.3 as an example.

The *root* node is A. The *degree* of a node is determined by the number of branches it has to other nodes. Nodes C and H have degree 2, nodes B and D have degree 1 and nodes E, F, G, I, J have degree 0. Nodes with degree 0 are

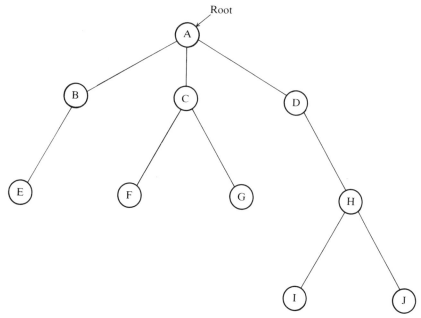

Figure 4.3   A general tree

called terminal or leaf nodes. Nodes that have a degree >0 (but excluding the root node) are called *branch* nodes. If nodes have the same parent, they are called *siblings*. The *ancestors* of a node are all the nodes on a path from the root to that node; e.g. the ancestors of I are A, D and H.

4.2   Binary trees

If, in a tree, the maximum number of branches from any one node is two, such a tree is called a *binary tree*. Binary trees have other differences from the general

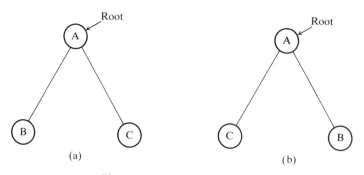

Figure 4.4   Ordered binary trees

tree as discussed earlier and these differences are covered by the following definition:

A binary tree *is a finite set of nodes, which is either empty or consists of a root together with a left subtree and a right subtree.*

Firstly, we allow a binary tree to be empty. Also a binary tree consisting of a single node is said to have an empty left subtree and an empty right subtree. Secondly, by differentiating between left and right subtrees we introduce the concept of an *ordered tree*. Figure 4.4 shows two *different* binary trees.

Obviously there are many different ways of describing trees. For example, we could make use of nested parentheses; e.g. we could specify the tree given in Fig. 4.3 by the following list:

$$(A\ (B\ (E),\ C\ (F\ ,\ G),\ D\ (H\ (I\ ,J)\ )\ )\ )$$

The root node is written first followed by a list of subtrees of that node. However, for the remainder of this text we describe all trees by drawing, as used in earlier illustrations, starting with the root node and drawing the branches downwards.

4.3   Tree representation in computer memory

As with drawing methods, trees may be represented in a computer memory in many different ways. We now consider a method of tree representation utilizing a multilink dynamic data structure. As with our approach to linked list representation, nodes can be obtained from a general pool as the tree grows and old nodes returned to the pool for re-use as the tree is pruned. The number of link fields required for any node is dependent on the degree of that node; however, for practical purposes we choose to illustrate binary tree representation. A typical binary tree node is shown in Fig. 4.5 and consists of three fields:

Field 1   to hold a pointer to a left subtree
Field 2   to hold an item of information (data)
Field 3   to hold a pointer to a right subtree

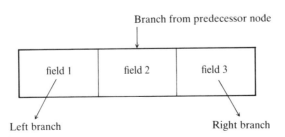

Figure 4.5   A typical node used in binary tree representation

Thus a complete binary tree representation consists of a pointer to the root node together with a set of branch nodes and a set of terminal nodes. If the pointer to the root contains a nil value then the tree is said to be empty. Figure 4.6 shows such a representation.

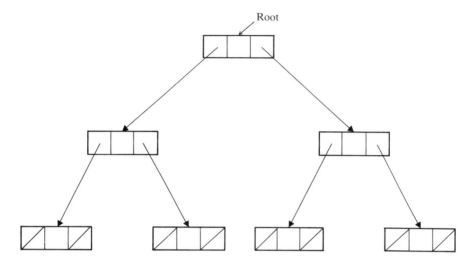

Figure 4.6   A possible data structure for binary tree representation

BUILDING A TREE REPRESENTATION IN MEMORY

Using the order relation between items of data as defined in Section 2.12 we now propose building a binary tree such that

1. data items in the left subtree of any node come before or are equal to the data item in that node and
2. data items in the right subtree of any node come after the data item in that node.

Thus, given the data items

$$F, C, A, D, K, G, Z$$

the resulting tree structure required to contain these items of data is shown in Fig. 4.7.

A binary tree as just described is known as a *binary search tree* and provides a very useful basic data structure for the design of tree processing algorithms. We first of all consider procedures for building a two-link data structure to represent a binary search tree.

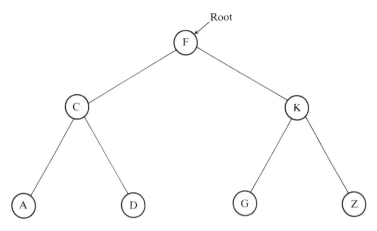

Figure 4.7   An ordered binary tree

We assume the following definitions:

$$\text{type link} = \uparrow\text{node};$$
$$\text{node} = \text{record}$$
$$\text{data:char;}$$
$$\text{1branch,rbranch:link}$$
$$\text{end;}$$

The following procedure, given a pointer to a tree together with an item of data, will create a new leaf containing the data item and insert this leaf into the tree with respect to the given ordering:

```
procedure GROWALEAF(var ptr:link;item:char);
begin
  if ptr = nil then
  begin
    new(ptr);
    ptr↑.data:= item;
    ptr↑.1branch:= nil;
    ptr↑.rbranch:= nil
  end
  else
  if item < =ptr↑.data then GROWALEAF(ptr↑.1branch,item)
                        else GROWALEAF(ptr↑.rbranch,item)
end;
```

We can now specify the actual tree building procedure which consists simply of repeated calls to GROWALEAF:

```
procedure BUILDBINARYSEARCHTREE;
begin
  root:= nil;
  readln(item);
  while item⟨⟩'?'do
  begin
    GROWALEAF(root,item);
    readln(item)
  end
end;
```

4.4   Program 9

Using the procedures just described this program, when given appropriate data, builds a two-link tree representation of a binary search tree in computer memory. As for linked lists, data consists of single characters and input is terminated by the character "?".

We normally build a tree structure in computer memory so that the data held in the tree may be processed in some way or other. We now investigate some tree processing operations; these operations all assume a binary search tree structure is available.

4.5   Searching a binary tree

This is the easiest of tree operations to do as we simply examine the root node and if it contains the item we are searching for the search is finished; otherwise we search the left subtree and then the right subtree. The following recursive procedure implements the search routine:

```
procedure TREESEARCH(ptr:link;item:char);
begin
  if ptr = nil then writeln('Item not in tree')
  else
  if ptr^.data = item then writeln('Item found')
  else
  if ptr^.data > item then TREESEARCH(ptr^.1branch,item)
                 else TREESEARCH(ptr^.rbranch,item)
end;
```

4.6   Inserting a node into a binary tree

Insertion of a node is quite simple: we follow a path down the tree until we come to the point of insertion and then link in the new node. We could, of course, start with an empty tree in which case insertion is simply a matter of planting the root. The non-recursive procedure makes use of two pointers named FIND and FOLLOW, such that as FIND moves around the tree looking for a place to insert the new node, FOLLOW follows one node behind. Thus when FIND comes to a nil pointer FOLLOW is pointing to the node *after* which insertion will take place. Figure 4.8 illustrates this method of node insertion when inserting a node whose data item is the integer 11.

We could just as easily have used the recursive procedure GROWALEAF defined earlier which carries out exactly the same task. However, this version of

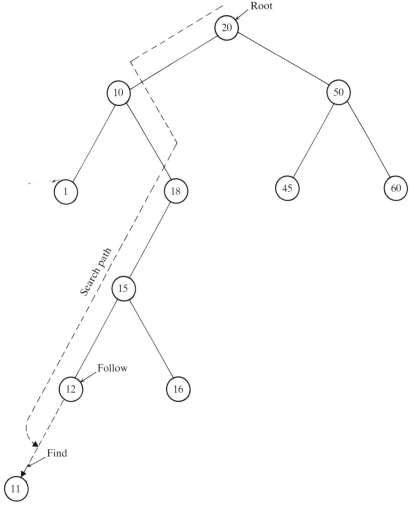

Figure 4.8   Node insertion into an ordered binary tree

node insertion is given in order to aid understanding of the non-recursive procedure for node deletion given in Section 4.7.

It is also interesting and worth while to compare the elegance of the recursive algorithm with its non-recursive version.

The insertion routine is implemented by the following procedure:

```
procedure INSERTLEAF(var ptr:link;item:char);
var find,follow.newleaf:link;
begin
  find := ptr;
  if ptr = nil then
  begin
    new(newleaf);
    newleaf↑.data := item;
    newleaf↑.lbranch := nil;
    newleaf↑.rbranch := nil;
    ptr := newleaf
  end
  else
  begin
    while find⟨ ⟩nil do
    begin
      follow := find;
      if item < = find↑.data then find := find↑.lbranch
                             else find := find↑.rbranch
    end;
    new(newleaf);
    if item <follow↑.data then
      follow↑.lbranch := newleaf
    else
      follow↑.rbranch := newleaf;
    newleaf↑.data := item;
    newleaf↑.lbranch := nil;
    newleaf↑.rbranch := nil
  end
end;
```

4.7 Deletion of a node from a binary tree

Deletion of a node from a binary tree is rather more difficult than the operations of searching and inserting. The deletion algorithm is as follows:

Search the tree to find the node to be deleted.

Replace the deleted node by its right subtree and put the left subtree of the deleted node as the leftmost node of the right subtree of the deleted node.

To clarify the deletion algorithm we follow through its execution when deleting the node B from the tree given in Fig. 4.9. We assume the search part of the algorithm to be completed and the pointer FIND to be pointing to node B.

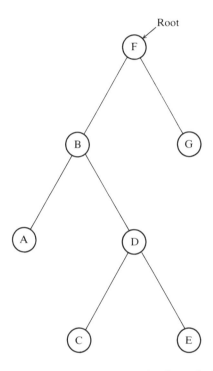

Figure 4.9   The binary tree referred to for node deletion

To delete the node and replace it by its right subtree we change the pointer in the predecessor of B (see Fig. 4.10). The broken line shows that changing the pointer removes not only the node B but also removes the left subtree of B. However, we can still reference this subtree by means of the pointer FIND. Using the pointer FOLLOW, a path is traced out to the leftmost node of the right subtree of the deleted node (see Fig. 4.11). Finally, we can now attach the left subtree of the deleted node to the node pointed at by FOLLOW (see Fig. 4.12 on page 82).

The final revised tree structure is given in Fig. 4.13 and it can be seen that the tree has been pruned as required and the pruned tree still maintains the specified ordering. It should be carefully noted that the deletion algorithm assumes that the node to be deleted is in the initial tree.

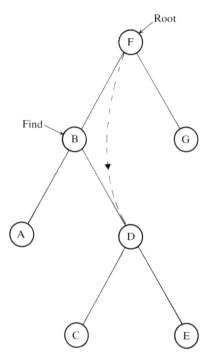

Figure 4.10 Node deletion—stage 1

A procedure to perform the deletion routine is now given:

```
procedure FINDANDDELETE(var ptr:link;item:char);
var find,follow,hold:link;
begin
  find:= ptr;
  if item = ptr↑.data then
  begin
    hold:= ptr↑.rbranch;
    if hold = nil then ptr:= ptr↑.lbranch
    else
    begin
      ptr:= hold;
      while hold↑.lbranch⟨ ⟩nil do hold:= hold↑.lbranch;
      hold↑.lbranch:= find↑.lbranch
    end
  end
  else
    begin
      while item⟨ ⟩find↑.data do
```

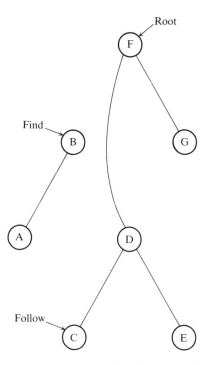

Figure 4.11   Node deletion—stage 2

```
begin
  follow := find;
  if item < find↑.data then find := find↑.lbranch
                        else find := find↑.rbranch
end;
hold := find↑.rbranch;
if hold = nil then
begin
  if follow↑.rbranch = find then follow↑.rbranch := hold
                             else follow↑.lbranch := hold;
  while hold↑.lbranch⟨ ⟩nil do hold := hold↑.lbranch;
  hold↑.lbranch := find↑.lbranch
end
else
if follow↑.rbranch = find then follow↑.rbranch := find↑.lbranch
                           else follow↑.lbranch := find↑.rbranch
        end
      end;
```

These procedures are used in Program 10.

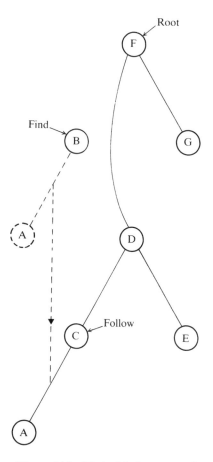

Figure 4.12   Node deletion—stage 3

4.8   Tree traversals

We now examine a group of operations on trees, known as tree *traversals*. A tree traversal simply means visiting each of the nodes of a given tree once. Obviously there are many different ways of doing this and some possible traversals are illustrated. In Fig. 4.14, visitation is indicated by the broken line passing *underneath a node*. (Note that references to the underneath, leftside and rightside of nodes are made assuming that tree diagrams, as viewed by the reader, are drawn in the conventional way, i.e. from the root downwards.)

We now investigate the various traversals possible when each node is visited as shown by the broken line in Fig. 4.15. The traversal starts at the root and follows the arrows on the broken line. Again assuming a visit to occur as the broken line passes underneath a node, we can see that the order of such

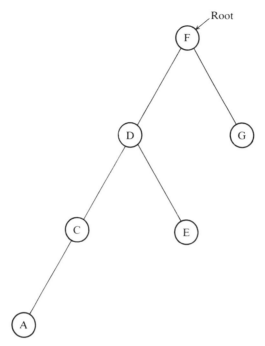

Figure 4.13   Tree after node deletion is completed

visitations, given by the numbers underneath each node, produces the sequence

A, B, C, D, E

Such a traversal is known as an *in-order* traversal. If a tree is built with the ordering constraints given for the procedure BUILDBINARYSEARCHTREE, an in-order traversal will always produce an ascending sequence of data items.

Because of the recursive nature of trees recursive algorithms are a natural choice for tree processing. An algorithm for the in-order traversal is now given.

4.9   Algorithm 21. An in-order tree traversal

```
inordertraversal(root)
begin
   if the tree is empty do nothing
   else
   begin
      inordertraversal(left subtree)
      output data at current node
      inordertraversal(right subtree)
   end
end
```

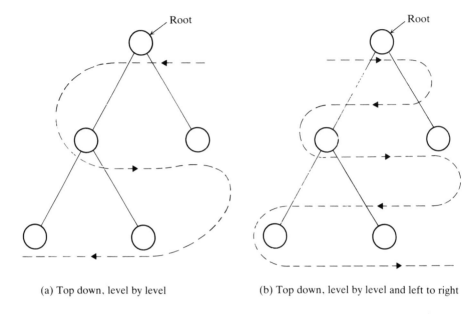

(a) Top down, level by level   (b) Top down, level by level and left to right

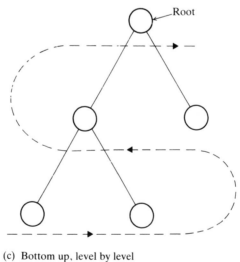

(c) Bottom up, level by level

Figure 4.14   Level-by-level tree traversals

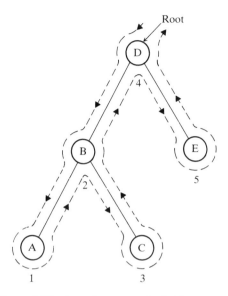

Figure 4.15 In-order traversal of a binary tree

We implement this algorithm by the following procedure:

```
procedure INORDER(ptr:link);
begin
if ptr⟨ ⟩nil then
    begin
        INORDER(ptr↑.lbranch);
        write(ptr↑.data:5);
        INORDER(ptr↑.rbranch)
    end
end;
```

To trace through a call of this procedure we take as an example the tree shown in Fig. 4.16.

The initial call will be INORDER(root) and the trace diagram (Fig. 4.17) shows the recursive calls together with the output.

If we now define a node visitation to occur when a node is passed on its left-hand side by the broken line, the order of node vistations is obviously changed. The numbers to the left of each node in Fig. 4.18 show the new order of node visitations producing the sequence

$$D, B, A, C, E$$

This traversal is known as a *pre-order* traversal and is implemented by the following algorithm.

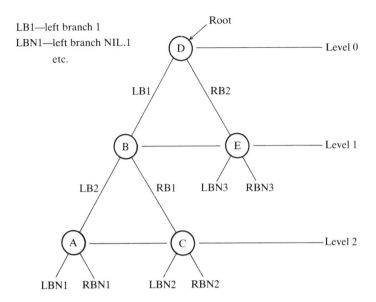

Figure 4.16 A labelled ordered binary tree. The labels refer to the actual parameters of the procedure calls indicated in Figs 4.17, 4.20 and 4.21

4.10   Algorithm 22. A pre-order traversal

preordertraversal(root)
begin
    if the tree is empty then do nothing
    else
    begin
        output data at current node
        preordertraversal(left subtree)
        preordertraversal(right subtree)
    end
end

We examine one more tree traversal. In this traversal a node visitation occurs when a node is passed on its rightside by the broken line. As before we indicate the order of node visitations by numbers, this time on the right-hand side of each node (see Fig. 4.19).

The sequence produced by this final traversal is

A, C, B, E, D

This traversal is called a *post-order* traversal.

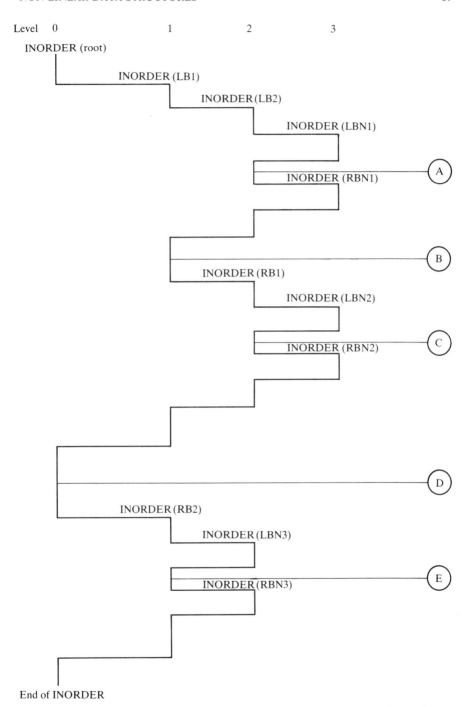

Figure 4.17 A trace of the in-order procedure calls showing the levels of recursion

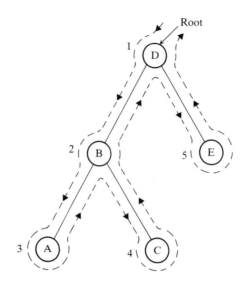

Figure 4.18   Pre-order traversal of a binary tree

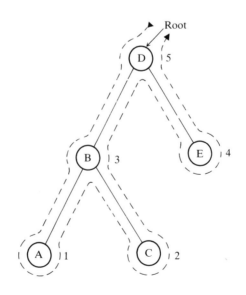

Figure 4.19   Post-order traversal of a binary tree

4.11 Algorithm 23. A post-order traversal

```
postordertraversal(root)
begin
  if the tree is empty then do nothing
  else
  begin
    postordertraversal(left subtree)
    postordertraversal(right subtree)
    output data at current node
  end
end
```

Algorithms 22 and 23 are implemented by the following procedures:

```
procedure PREORDER(ptr:link);
begin
  if ptr⟨ ⟩nil then
  begin
    write(ptr↑.data:5);
    PREORDER(ptr↑.lbranch);
    PREORDER(ptr↑.rbranch)
  end
end;

procedure POSTORDER(ptr:link);
begin
  if ptr⟨ ⟩nil then
  begin
    POSTORDER(ptr↑.lbranch);
    POSTORDER(ptr↑.rbranch);
    write(ptr↑.data:5)
  end
end;
```

To enable the reader to follow through calls on these last two procedures, trace diagrams are given in Figs 4.20 and 4.21.

4.12 Program 10

A menu driven program utilizes all the tree operation procedures defined. The program allows the user to choose any of the following:

1. Build a binary search tree
2. Perform in-order, pre-order and post-order traversals
3. Insert and delete nodes

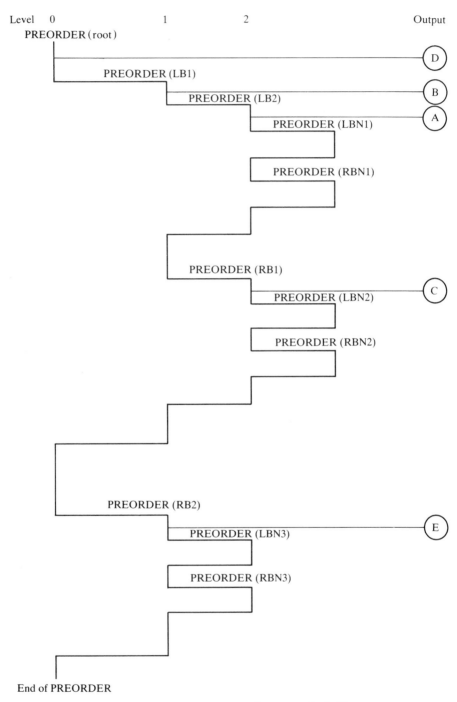

Figure 4.20   A trace during a pre-order traversal of a binary tree

Level   0   1   2   Output

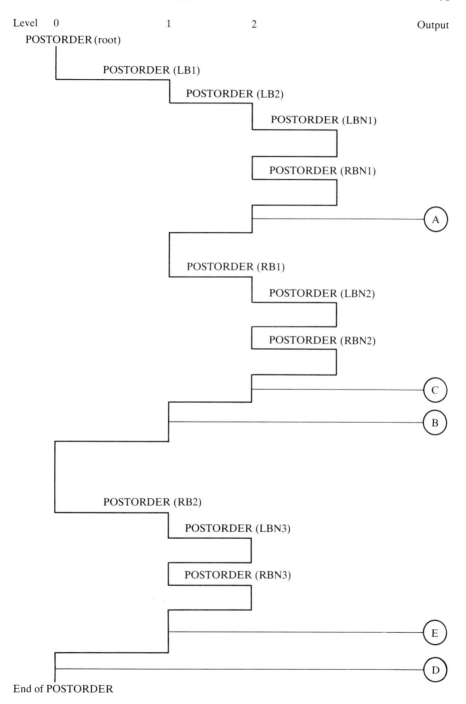

Figure 4.21   A trace during a post-order traversal of a binary tree

The reader should experiment with this program, building trees and observing the result of different traversals. We will return to tree traversals and their uses in later sections of the book.

4.13   Graphs and linked lists

We first introduce in simple terms the concept of a *graph*. A graph G consists of two sets V and E. V is a non-empty, finite set of vertices and E is a set of pairs of vertices representing the edges of the graph. The graph G1 is defined as follows:

$$V(G1) = \{1, 2, 3, 4\} \qquad \text{(the set of vertices)}$$
$$E(G1) = \{(1,2), (1,3), (2,4), (1,4)\} \text{ (the set of edges)}$$

A drawing of graph G1 is given in Fig. 4.22.

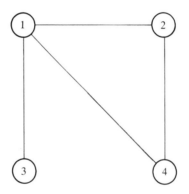

Figure 4.22   An undirected graph

Graphs are classed as *directed* graphs or *undirected* graphs. In an undirected graph the pairs (v1,v2) and (v2,v1) represent the same edge; therefore the set

$$E1(G1) = \{(2,1), (3,1), (4,2), (4,1)\}$$

is equivalent to the original set of edges E(G1), given for G1. In a directed graph the pairs of vertices representing the edges are *ordered*. The first member of such an ordered pair we call the *source* of the edge and the second member of the pair we call the *destination* of the edge. Ordered pairs are indicated by the use of square brackets. Thus [v1,v2] and [v2,v1] are ordered pairs and represent *different* edges. Figure 4.23 shows the directed graph G2 where

$$V(G2) = \{1, 2, 3, 4\}$$
$$E(G2) = \{[1,2], [2,3], [3,4], [1,4]\}$$

The edges of a directed graph are drawn with an arrow pointing from the source vertex to the destination vertex.

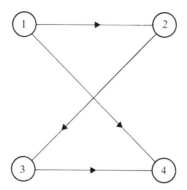

Figure 4.23   A directed graph

4.14   Representation of a directed graph in computer memory

There are many ways of representing a graph in a computer memory and we
now investigate one of these, the method of *adjacency lists*. For any given vertex
V_i in a directed graph, there exists a list of adjacent vertices to V_i. Vertex V_j is
said to be adjacent to vertex V_i if V_j is the destination vertex of an arc joining V_i
and V_j. If V_i is not the source vertex for any area then it is said to have an empty
adjacency list.

Figure 4.24 shows part of a directed graph and from this it can be seen that the
vertices V_j and V_k are adjacent to the vertex V_i. We can also observe that the
lists of adjacent vertices to V_j and V_k are empty lists. Thus using the concept of
adjacency lists we can make a full description of the graph given in Fig. 4.23.

Vertex	Lists of adjacent vertices
1	2, 4
2	3
3	4
4	empty

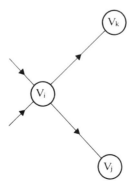

Figure 4.24   Adjacent vertices in a directed graph

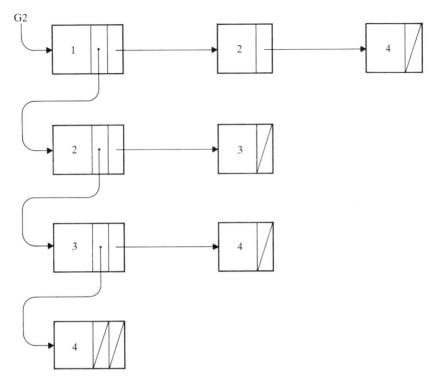

Figure 4.25   An adjacency list data structure representing the directed graph given in Fig. 4.23

Using the adjacency list description of a graph together with our knowledge of linked lists, the following data structure can be used to represent a graph in computer memory. The vertices of the graph form a linked list and each node of this list contains

1. The vertex label
2. A link to the next vertex
3. A link to the adjacency list associated with the vertex labelled in 1

Figure 4.25 illustrates such a data structure representation for the graph G2 (see Fig. 4.23).

To build a data structure as just described is only a matter of reading the number of vertices together with the set of ordered pairs defining their connectivities and then applying the various list processing procedures as previously defined, albeit with different more appropriate names.

Assuming the following declarations and definitions:

        type   link1 = ↑vnode;
               link2 = ↑anode;

```
                        vnode = record
                                  vernum:integer;
                                  nextv:link1;
                                  adjlist:link2
                                end;
                        anode = record
                                  vernum:integer;
                                  nexta:link2
                                end;
              var graph,index,ivertex,newvertex:link1;
                  ver1,ver2,nov:integer;
                  newadj:link2;
```

we can define the following procedures needed to build a graph data structure:

```
              procedure BUILDGRAPH;
              var i:integer;
              begin
              graph:= nil;
                writeln('How many vertices');
                readln(nov);
                for i:= nov downto 1 do
                begin
                  new(newvertex);
                  newvertex↑.vernum:= i;
                  newvertex↑.nextv:= graph;
                  newvertex↑.adjlist:= nil;
                  graph:= newvertex
                end;
                writeln('Input ordered pairs');
                readln(ver1,ver2);
                repeat
                  SEARCHFORVERTEX(graph,ver1);
                  UPDATEVERTEX(index,ver2);
                  writeln('Next ordered pair');
                  readln(ver1,ver2)
                until (ver1 = 0)and(ver2 = 0)
              end;
          procedure SEARCHFORVERTEX(ptr:link1;vnum:integer);
          begin
            if ptr⟨ ⟩nil then
            if ptr↑.vernum = vnum then index:= ptr
            else
            SEARCHFORVERTEX(ptr↑.nextv,vnum)
          end;
```

```
procedure UPDATEVERTEX(ptr:linkl;vnum:integer);
begin
  new(newadj);
  newadj↑.vernum := vnum;
  newadj↑.nexta := ptr^.adjlist
  ptr↑.adjlist := newadj
end;
```

The procedure BUILDGRAPH first of all builds a linked list of vertices using their vertex number as a label and then, as each ordered pair is read, the appropriate adjacency list is updated.

4.15 Partial orderings

Given the set of vertices

$$V = \{1, 2, 3\}$$

we can see that a complete set of ordered pairs is given by

$$E = \{[1,2],[2,1],[1,3],[3,1],[2,3],[3,2]\}$$

and the corresponding graph is shown in Fig. 4.26.

If we imagine ourselves following the edges in the directions specified by the arrows, it is fairly obvious that we could go on following cyclic paths in the graph forever.

We now proceed to examine a class of graphs whose sets of ordered pairs are not complete but reveal only a partial ordering. We understand partial ordering to mean that there exists no cyclic paths in the graph. A graph with partial ordering is given in Fig. 4.27.

Graphs belonging to this class can be drawn in linear form such that all edge directions are to the right (see Fig. 4.28). Thus the linear sequence obtained for a partial ordering shows each vertex preceding any of its adjacent vertices. Sorting the vertices of a partial ordering into a linear form as just described is known as *topological sorting* and can be accomplished by the following algorithm.

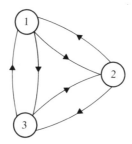

Figure 4.26   A totally ordered graph

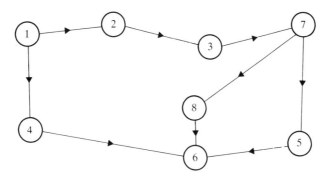

Figure 4.27 A partially ordered or acyclic graph

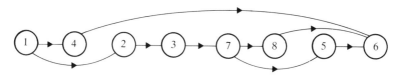

Figure 4.28 The linear form of the graph given in Fig. 4.27

4.16 Algorithm 24. A topological sort

```
topologicalsort(graph)
begin
repeat
    pick any vertex which has no predecessors
    output its label
    delete this vertex from the graph together
        with all edges leading from it
until graph is empty
end
```

We illustrate the execution of this algorithm by applying it to the graph given in Fig. 4.29.

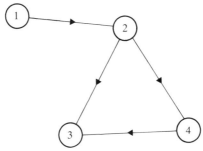

Figure 4.29 The partially ordered graph referred to in the text illustrating topological sorting

We choose vertex 1 (the only possible one in this graph) as the starting point. Output the label 1 and delete vertex 1 from the graph, leaving the graph as follows:

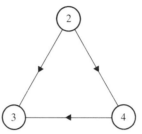

Again only one choice is possible—vertex 2. Output the label 2 and delete vertex 2 from the graph, leaving

Next we choose vertex 4, leaving ③

The final choice is vertex 3 and the topologically sorted vertex labels are given by the output sequence

$$1, 2, 4, 3$$

We can see that the algorithm gives the order of vertices we would have obtained if the graph had been drawn originally in linear form.

To implement Algorithm 24 we need only to amend the initial concept of graph representation by adjacency lists. We add to each node in the vertex list a field containing the number of edges leading into it.

Given the graph shown in Fig. 4.30, the 'edges in' count is as follows:

Vertex	Edges in
1	0
2	1
3	2
4	1
5	1

Figure 4.31 shows the data structure used to represent the above graph. This structure is needed by the topological sort algorithm.

We make use of the 'edges in' count to find a starting point for the topological sort by searching the vertex list for a vertex containing a zero count. If such a vertex cannot be found, the sort cannot be performed. If a vertex with a zero count is found, its label is printed out and the vertex removed from the graph as follows. The vertex is deleted from the vertex list and its adjacency list is then used to amend the 'edges in' count of all its adjacent vertices.

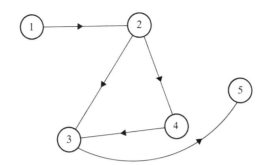

Figure 4.30 A sample acyclic graph

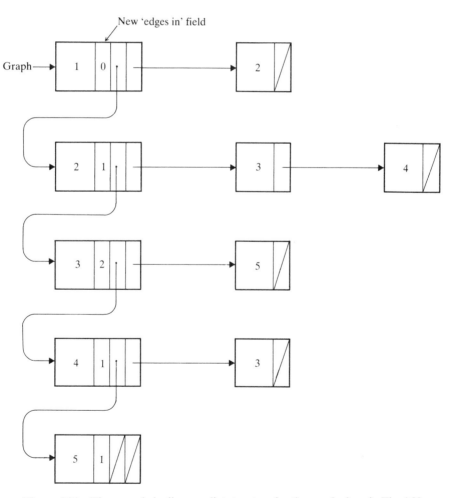

Figure 4.31 The amended adjacency list structure for the graph given in Fig. 4.30

Using the graph representation in Fig. 4.32 the following transformations are made to the structure:

Step 1. (a) Vertex with zero 'edges in' count has label 1; output this label.
      (b) Remove from structure and amend 'edges in' count of all vertices in its adjacency list.

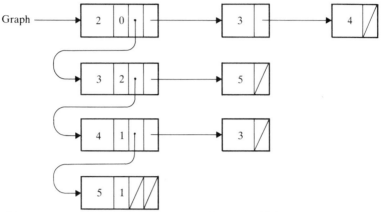

Step 2. (a) Vertex with zero 'edges in' count has label 2; output this label.
      (b) Remove from structure and amend 'edges in' count of all vertices in its adjacency list.

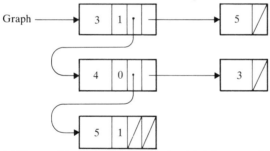

Step 3. (a) Vertex with zero 'edges in' count has label 4; output this label.
      (b) Remove from structure and amend 'edges in' count of all vertices in its adjacency list.

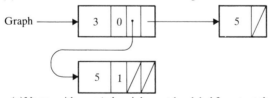

Step 4. (a) Vertex with zero 'edges in' count has label 3; output this label.
      (b) Remove from structure and amend 'edges in' count of all vertices in its adjacency list.

Graph ⟶ | 5 | 0 |⧄|

Step 5. (a) Vertex with zero 'edges in' count has label 5; output this label.
      (b) Remove from structure and amend 'edges in' count of all vertices in its adjacency list.

Graph ⟶ nil

Step 6. Graph is empty. Therefore algorithm terminates giving the topologically sorted vertices as

1, 2, 4, 3, 5

4.17   Program 11

This program allows input of any graph representing a partial ordering. A topological sort is then executed on the graph. Input consists of the number of vertices followed by the set of ordered pairs representing edges. Termination of input is by the ordered pair $(0, 0)$.

TASKS AND PARTIAL ORDERINGS

We now let the vertices in a graph representing a partial ordering stand for tasks to be performed and the edges to represent precedence relationships between these tasks; i.e. given the following graph:

we interpret this as meaning task 2 can only be carried out *after* tasks 1 and 3. Alternatively, we can say tasks 1 and 3 take *precedence* over task 2. There is no precedence relationship between tasks 1 and 3 and so they may be carried out in any order.

Application of Algorithm 24 to this graph gives the following linear ordering:

$$3, 1, 2$$

Obviously there is a second possible ordering, i.e.

$$1, 3, 2$$

Thus we can see that a topological sort gives the order in which the tasks may be carried out.

A second very simple illustrative example is drawn from the precedence of operations in arithmetic. Given the following classes of operators:

Relational   (R)
Adding   (A)
Multiply   (M)
Negation   (N)

we can represent their precedence relationships by means of the following graph:

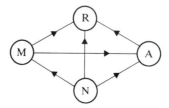

A topological sort gives the following linear order of vertices:

N, M, A, R

(in this case the only possible ordering). Therefore, if an expression contained these four classes of operators then they must be performed in the order given.

Finally, we examine a more realistic example. Suppose that in a particular organization a certificate of merit is awarded to people who obtain a set of badges where each badge is obtained by the completion of a study task. Certain badges must be obtained before others, i.e. there are specific precedence relationships between some badges and these are given in the following table:

Badge award	Badge number	Badges required first
Numeracy	1	None
Local history	2	Books
Camping	3	Numeracy, first aid
Cycling	4	First aid
Outdoor activities	5	Cycling, swimming
Swimming	6	None
Age concern	7	First aid, local history
Handicrafts	8	Numeracy
Local government	9	Local history, books
Indoor activities	10	Numeracy
Books	11	None
First aid	12	None

Figure 4.32 shows the above table of tasks and relationships as a partial ordering in which the vertices are labelled with the badge numbers and the edges represent the precedence relationships between badges.

Application of Algorithm 24 to the graph gives the following sequence of badge tasks:

12, 11, 6, 4, 5, 2, 9, 7, 1, 10, 8, 3

To gain a certificate of merit the badges may be obtained in this topologically sorted order.

As mentioned earlier, there can often be more than one solution and in the above example different solutions can be obtained as any one of the tasks 1, 6 or 11 can be used as the starting vertex.

4.18 Paths through a graph

Given any directed graph representing a partial ordering, if there exists an edge [v1,v2], we can say that there is a path from v1 to v2. If in the same graph there

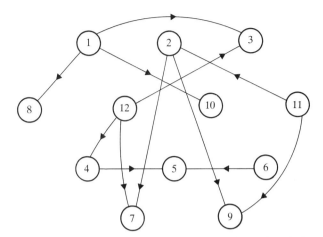

Figure 4.32 A graphical representation of the badge tasks relationships

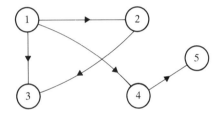

Figure 4.33 A simple acyclic graph illustrating paths

is also an edge [v2,v3], we can say that there is a path from v1 to v3 passing through v2. We are given a graph G as shown in Fig. 4.33.

If we choose vertex 1 as a starting point then we can list all the paths through G thus:

$$1 \rightarrow 2 \rightarrow 3$$
$$1 \rightarrow 3$$
$$1 \rightarrow 4 \rightarrow 5$$

4.19 A building project

We now examine the various activities that occur during a small building project. We specify activities in terms of reaching goals (events) as shown below:

Event 1   Project commences
Event 2   Completion of foundations
Event 3   Completion of walls
Event 4   Completion of floors
Event 5   Windows and doors fixed
Event 6   Completion of painting
Event 7   Completion of boundary walls
Event 8   Site cleared and paths completed

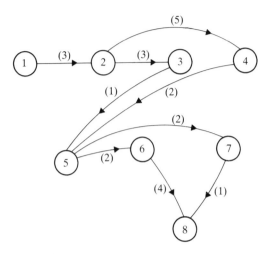

Figure 4.34   An event/activity graph

We also know that some activities can only happen sequentially while others can occur concurrently. The order of activities is illustrated by an event/activity graph (see Fig. 4.34).

Events are represented by vertices and activities by edges. The time, in days, taken for each activity is written, parenthesized, on the appropriate edge. Where two or more edges have the same source vertex, the activities represented by those edges can be carried out concurrently. We can observe that the *minimum* time taken to complete the project is given by the *longest* path (measured in days) from the start event to the finish event. This path is known as the *critical path* through the graph. For any such project it is possible to have more than one critical path. Activities that lie on this critical path are known as *critical activities*; if critical activity times can be shortened then the project can be completed more quickly. This method of analysis, using graph representations, has been successfully applied to many large building/engineering projects.

Referring to the graph shown in Fig. 4.34 and applying Program 11 we see that all paths through the graph are as follows:

$$1 \rightarrow 2 \rightarrow 4 \rightarrow 5 \rightarrow 7 \rightarrow 8$$
Pathlength = 13

$$1 \rightarrow 2 \rightarrow 4 \rightarrow 5 \rightarrow 6 \rightarrow 8$$
Pathlength = 16

$$1 \rightarrow 2 \rightarrow 3 \rightarrow 5 \rightarrow 7 \rightarrow 8$$
Pathlength = 10

$$1 \rightarrow 2 \rightarrow 3 \rightarrow 5 \rightarrow 6 \rightarrow 8$$
Pathlength = 13

The critical path is path 2 and from examination we see that the critical activities are:

Laying the foundations
Laying the floors
Fixing doors and windows
Painting
Site clearance and laying paths

As mentioned, shortening any of the critical activity times can reduce the length of the critical path, but it must be borne in mind in that in doing so other critical paths may be created.

4.20 A travel problem

Given a graph G shown in Fig. 4.35, we observe the existence of three paths from vertex 1 to vertex 5:

Path 1	$1 \rightarrow 2 \rightarrow 5$
Path 2	$1 \rightarrow 3 \rightarrow 4 \rightarrow 5$
Path 3	$1 \rightarrow 4 \rightarrow 5$

If the edges in the graph are all assumed to be of unit length, it is obvious that the shortest paths are paths 1 and 3. Each of these paths involves three vertices. However, if the paths are of different lengths (often referred to as weighted path lengths), the paths passing through the smallest number of vertices are not necessarily the shortest paths. Figure 4.36 illustrates a weighted path version of the graph given in Fig. 4.35. The weightings are shown parenthesized on each edge.

Again we observe the following paths from vertex 1 to vertex 5:

Path 1 $1 \rightarrow 2 \rightarrow 5$ pathlength = 6
Path 2 $1 \rightarrow 3 \rightarrow 4 \rightarrow 5$ pathlength = 3
Path 3 $1 \rightarrow 4 \rightarrow 5$ pathlength = 8

We now see that the shortest path is the path that passes through the most vertices (path 2). Maps showing towns connected by roads or maps showing rail

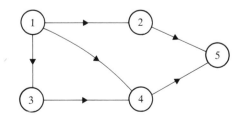

Figure 4.35   Unit length paths in a graph

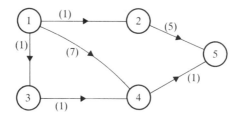

Figure 4.36   Weighted length paths in a graph

systems such as the London Underground can be represented by graphs similar to that in Fig. 4.36. Given such a map representation, a traveller may wish to know:

1. whether paths exist between two given places and
2. if they do, which is the shortest path.

In order to demonstrate such applications of graphs the procedure FINDALLPATHS given in Program 12 makes use of an amended version of

Figure 4.37   Amended adjacency list representation for part of the graph given in Fig. 4.36

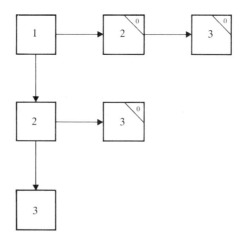

Figure 4.38   Skeletal adjacency list representation of a graph

the adjacency list representation and charts all possible paths through any graph from a given vertex. The adjacency list shown in Fig. 4.31 is amended as follows. Each node in the list of adjacent vertices now contains

1. the number of the adjacent vertex,
2. the path weighting of the adjacent vertex,
3. a flag field (for use when tracing paths through the graph) and
4. a link to the next adjacent vertex.

For example, the amended adjacency list for vertex 1 of the graph given in Fig. 4.36 is shown in Fig. 4.37.

The procedure FINDALLPATHS works as follows. We are given the skeletal adjacency list representation in Fig. 4.38 (flag fields are shown in the top right-hand corner of nodes).

We imagine a pointer moving around the structure as follows. Given a path start vertex (say vertex 1), the pointer first of all finds this vertex. If the given start vertex has an empty adjacency list, obviously there are no paths from this vertex and the procedure terminates. However, in the example given this is not the case and so we proceed as follows:

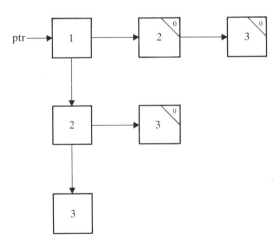

1. A copy of the pointer is pushed to a stack:

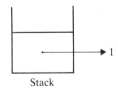

Stack

2. The pointer now moves to the first node of the adjacency list. The vertex that this node represents must lie on a path from vertex 1 and so its flag is set:

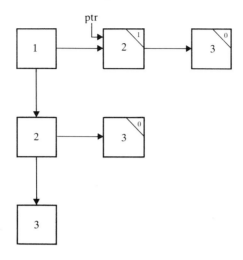

3. The vertex list is now searched for a node representing this vertex.

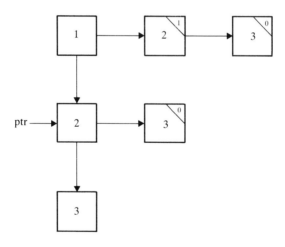

Steps 1 and 2 are repeated, giving:

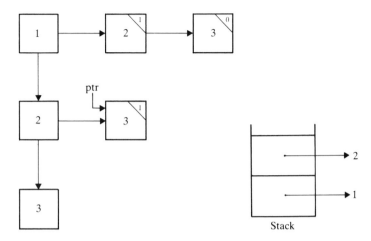

Repeating steps 3 and 1 we get:

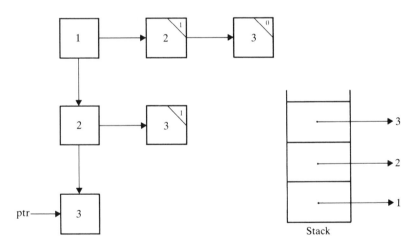

This time the pointer finds a vertex with an empty adjacency list. This signals the end of one particular path through the graph. When this occurs the vertices referenced by the stack of pointers lie on a path through the graph, this path is noted and the stack popped. The pointer then backtracks the path looking for an alternative path. This is done by examining the adjacency list of the vertex referenced by the current stack top element, for any unflagged nodes (initially this will be the penultimate vertex of the first path found). If an unflagged node is found, it indicates an alternative path and the path tracing process restarts from that point. If, however, no unflagged nodes are found, reference to the current vertex is popped from the stack and the flag fields of all its adjacency list nodes reset. By repeating this process we can see how alternate paths are built in sequence on the stack. If at any time the pointer backtracks to the starting vertex and finds no further unflagged nodes in its adjacency list then the procedure FINDALLPATHS terminates.

4.21 Program 12

This program is designed to output all the paths and path lengths through a graph representing a partial ordering. It was used to obtain the paths and pathlengths given in the examples in Sections 4.19 and 4.20. Input consists of the number of vertices followed by the set of ordered pairs representing edges together with a weighting factor for each edge. No test is made for cyclic paths in the graph. As before, input is terminated by the ordered pair (0, 0). This program can easily be amended for use with graphs that have non-weighted paths simply by initializing all weighting fields in adjacency list nodes to contain the value 1. The lines in the program requesting path weightings can then be omitted. (Note that the stack of pointers tracing out the various paths also contains the path weighting for each vertex. Once a path is terminated these weightings are summed to give the total path length.)

4.22 Problem set 3

1. Write procedures to perform the following tasks:
   (a) Make a copy of an existing binary tree.
   (b) Test two binary trees for equality. (Note that binary trees are said to be equal if they contain the same data items and have the same topological ordering.)
2. A catalogue of files in an operating system is organized as a binary search tree, according to the file names. Each file entry also contains the date on which the file was last accessed. The data is encoded as an integer, e.g. 880625 denotes 25 June 1988. In a program write and test Pascal procedures which respectively
   (a) update the last access date of a given file,
   (b) print out the names of all files whose last access date was before a given date.
3. Write a procedure that reads the following list of Pascal keywords from a text file and stores them in a binary search tree:

   IF,THEN,ELSE,DO,WHILE,BEGIN,END,VAR,TYPE,CONST,
   RECORD,WITH,CASE,PROGRAM

   Write a second procedure that, given a word and a pointer to the search tree, tests to see if the word is one of the given Pascal keywords or not and writes out some appropriate message. Test these procedures in a program.
4. Rewrite the library program (Program 8) so that the names of authors are stored in a binary search tree. Each author node will contain a pointer to a

subsidiary binary search tree in which the names of books attributed to the author are held. A skeletal outline of such a data structure is shown below:

Author tree   Pointers to book trees

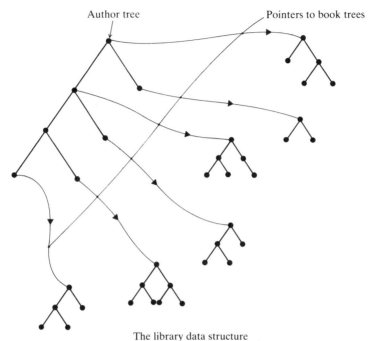

The library data structure

5. If the single character data items, A,B,C,D,E,F,G, are inserted in an empty binary search tree in alphabetical order, the tree degenerates into the following structure:

Root

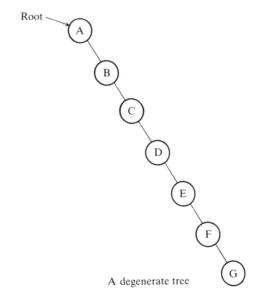

A degenerate tree

It is obvious that searching such a tree for the data item 'G' requires seven node comparisons while searching for the data item 'A' requires only one node comparison, giving a high average search time. Such a tree is said to be unbalanced. If the data items are input in the following sequence, D,F,B,E,G,A,C, a more balanced tree would be formed:

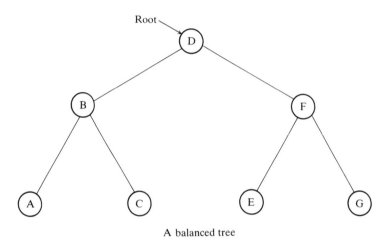

A balanced tree

When inputting data the chances of getting a balanced tree are greater if the items are inserted in a random order. Investigate this claim by writing a program that outputs some graphical representation of a tree and then uses it to experiment with different input sequences for a given set of data items.

6. An alternative method to the adjacency list method for representing directed graphs is the use of an adjacency matrix. In its simplest form an adjacency matrix is constructed as follows. For a graph consisting of N nodes we use an N by N matrix. If in the graph there exists an edge, say from node A to node B, the element indexed by [A,B] in the adjacency matrix would be set to true. For example, given the directed graph:

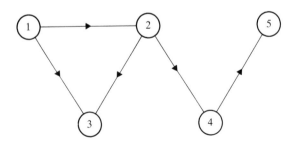

its adjacency matrix would be as follows:

Source vertex \ Destination vertex	1	2	3	4	5
1		T	T		
2			T	T	
3					
4					T
5					

It is fairly obvious that in many graphs with N nodes the edge count is likely to be much nearer N than $N * N$, thus giving a sparse adjacency matrix. If this is the case, such a matrix can be stored as a linked list.

Write a program to represent a directed graph by the adjacency matrix method where the matrix is stored as a linked list. Include in the program a procedure to write out all the paths through the graph from a given node. One of the parameters to this procedure will be a pointer to the linked list representing the adjacency matrix.

You can assume that the graph represents a partial ordering or alternatively you can include a check for cyclic paths in the graph.

7. Given the following expression representing the generalized list L:

$$L = (a, (d, (f, g), e), b, c)$$

write procedures to
(a) build a suitable data structure representation,
(b) make a copy of this structure.

PART TWO

Definition of language and the application of dynamic data structures

5

An introduction to language definition

5.1 A language generator

In a natural language such as English we have rules which guide us in the building up of sentences. Sentences are made up of phrases and we have rules governing the way phrases are put together to make bigger phrases, which in turn are put together to make sentences. These rules are known as the rules of *grammar* (or syntax). The following grammar defines a fragment of the English language:

$$
\begin{aligned}
\langle \text{sentence} \rangle &\rightarrow \langle \text{nounphrase} \rangle \langle \text{verbphrase} \rangle \\
\langle \text{nounphrase} \rangle &\rightarrow \text{the} \langle \text{noun} \rangle \\
\langle \text{verbphrase} \rangle &\rightarrow \langle \text{verb} \rangle \langle \text{nounphrase} \rangle \\
\langle \text{noun} \rangle &\rightarrow \langle \text{adjective} \rangle \langle \text{noun} \rangle \\
\langle \text{noun} \rangle &\rightarrow \text{boy} \\
\langle \text{noun} \rangle &\rightarrow \text{apple} \\
\langle \text{verb} \rangle &\rightarrow \text{ate} \\
\langle \text{verb} \rangle &\rightarrow \text{threw} \\
\langle \text{adjective} \rangle &\rightarrow \text{small} \\
\langle \text{adjective} \rangle &\rightarrow \text{large}
\end{aligned}
$$

Each line of the grammar is a rule involving a left-hand side, an arrow and a right-hand side. Left- and right-hand sides consist of two types of symbols. The first type, shown in angle brackets, is called a *non-terminal* symbol and the second type, shown in plain, is called a *terminal* symbol. Terminal symbols are the words of the language and non-terminal symbols refer to the types of phrases used in building up sentences of the language. There is a special non-terminal symbol and in our example this is the symbol ⟨sentence⟩. Such a grammar can be interpreted as a mechanism for generating sentences and one way of using it for this purpose is as follows.

5.2   A grammar as a language generator mechanism

1. Write down the special non-terminal symbol.
2. Repeat the following steps:
   (a) choose a non-terminal in the current line and choose some rule with that non-terminal on the left-hand side; then
   (b) replace the non-terminal with the right-hand side of the chosen rule.
3. Continue until there are no non-terminals in the current line.

   The following example will help to clarify the sequence of events:

1. ⟨sentence⟩
2(a). There is only one rule with ⟨sentence⟩ on the left-hand side, so replacing ⟨sentence⟩ with the right-hand side of that rule.
   (b). ⟨nounphrase⟩⟨verbphrase⟩
3(a). We now choose either of the non-terminals in the current line; it does not matter which one.

   For convenience we work from left to right.
   (b). the⟨noun⟩⟨verbphrase⟩

Repeating steps 2(a) and 2(b) we get the following sequence of substitutions:

the⟨adjective⟩⟨noun⟩⟨verbphrase⟩
the small⟨noun⟩⟨verbphrase⟩
the small boy⟨verb⟩⟨nounphrase⟩
the small boy ate⟨nounphrase⟩
the small boy ate the⟨noun⟩
the small boy ate the apple

The grammar given consists of a finite number of rules and a finite number of terminal symbols, yet it generates an infinite number of sentences (a language). The ability of our grammar to do this lies in the use of recursion in the rule for ⟨noun⟩; i.e.

$$\langle noun \rangle \rightarrow \langle adjective \rangle \langle noun \rangle$$

5.3   Representing a grammar in computer memory

We now consider the representation of our grammar in a computer by means of a complex data structure similar to that used in the library problem (see Section 3.29). An outline of a possible data structure is given in Fig. 5.1.

To implement such a structure we make the following definitions:

```
type string = packed array[1 . . 10]of char;
     tornt = (t,nt);{terminal or non-terminal}
     ruleptr = ↑rulenode;
     symptr = ↑symnode;
```

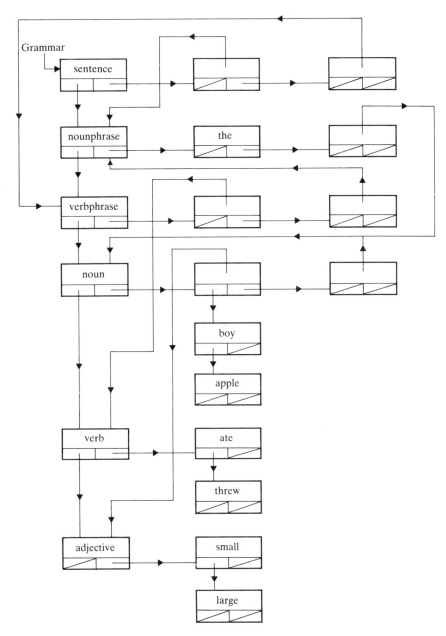

Figure 5.1 A possible structure representing the grammar given in the text

```
rulenode = record
              lhs:string;
              entry:symptr;
              link:ruleptr
           end;

symnode = record
              alt,link:symptr;
              case class:tornt of
                 t:(word:string);
                 nt:(rule:ruleptr)
           end;
```

Figure 5.2 shows a small part of the data structure in more detail.

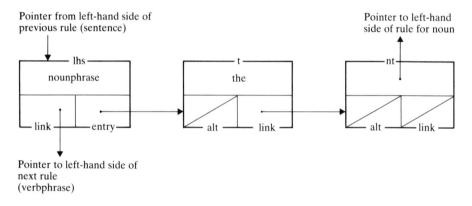

Figure 5.2   A detailed view of that part of the grammar data structure representing the rule for nounphrase

Creation of the grammar structure as described is straightforward and can be found in procedure BUILDGRAMMAR of Program 13.

We can see how nodes are assigned to the left-hand side of each rule. These nodes are pointed to by pointer variables whose names are:

srule
nprule
vprule
nrule
vrule
arule

A linked list of the left-hand side of all rules is then constructed:

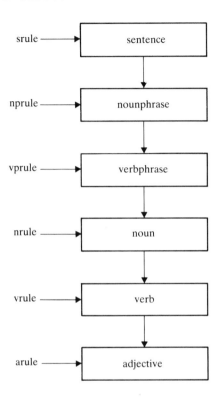

The rest of the procedure builds the right-hand sides of rules and links them into the appropriate left-hand sides.

We now turn to designing an algorithm that makes use of the stored grammar in order to generate sentences.

5.4   Algorithm 25. A sentence generator

```
generatesentence(ptr)
begin
      set a pointer variable called rhsscan to point to
      the first node on the right-hand side of the
      rule pointed to by ptr.
      initialize a counter.
      count the number of alternatives.
      choose an alternative at random.
      while scan of rule is incomplete do
```

```
        begin
           if scanned symbol is a terminal then write it out
           else
           generatesentence(link2(ptr))
           advance scan
        end
     end
```

We implement Algorithm 25 by the following recursive procedure:

```
procedure GENSENTENCE(r:ruleptr);
var rhsscan:symptr;
    count,i,rn:integer;
begin
  rhsscan:= r↑.entry;
  count:= 1;
  while rhsscan↑.alt⟨ ⟩nil do
  begin
    count:= count+1;
    rhsscan:= rhsscan↑.alt
  end;
  rn:= RANDOM mod count;{RANDOM generates integers between 0 and
4095}
  rhsscan:= r↑.entry;
  for i:= 1 to rn do rhsscan:= rhsscan↑.alt;
  while rhsscan⟨ ⟩nil do
  begin
    if rhsscan↑.class = t then writeln(rhsscan↑.word)
    else
    GENSENTENCE(rhsscan↑.rule);
    rhsscan:= rhsscan↑.link
  end
end;
```

5.5   Program 13

This is a sentence generator. The program builds a data structure as described
for the given fragment of English. Input to the program consists of a seed for the
random number function together with the number of sentences required to be
generated.

5.6   Derivation trees

Referring to the grammar given for a fragment of English, see Section 5.1, we
now consider the problem of checking the legality of a given sentence. If the

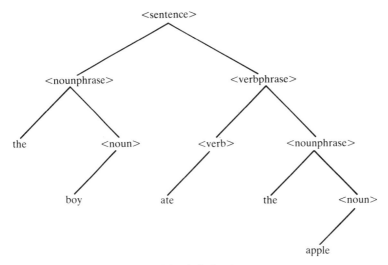

Figure 5.3   A derivation tree

given sentence can be derived by application of the rules given in Section 5.2, we say it is a legal sentence (syntactically correct). If it cannot be derived then it is illegal. We introduce the use of a general tree structure to illustrate the derivation stages of a given sentence. Figure 5.3 shows the *derivation tree* for the sentence, 'the boy ate the apple'.

Visiting the leaf nodes in left-to-right order shows the sentence has been derived and is therefore legal. We observe that each branch node, including the root node, represents the left-hand side of a rule and that its branch nodes in turn represent the right-hand side of that rule. Branch nodes are repeatedly drawn in this way until all leaf nodes contain the terminal symbols of a given sentence. If this is not possible, the derivation tree is incomplete, showing that the sentence cannot be generated and is therefore not legal.

An interesting feature of a derivation tree is that the leaves of any subtrees consisting of two or more nodes represent a phrase. We call such subtrees 'proper subtrees'. Thus the derivation tree of a sentence models the *phrase structure* of that sentence. Using the tree given in Fig. 5.3 we can see that all its proper subtrees are as shown in Fig. 5.4.

From Fig. 5.4 we can see that our sample sentence contains the following phrases:

(a) the boy
(b) ate the apple
(c) boy
(d) ate
(e) the apple
(f) apple

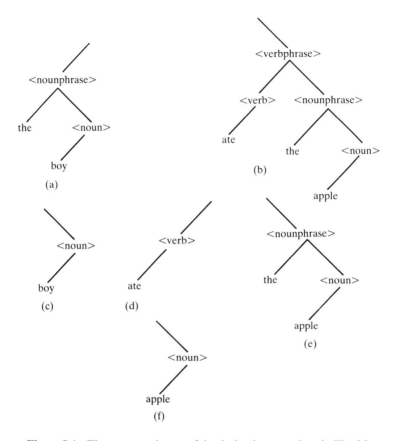

Figure 5.4   The proper subtrees of the derivation tree given in Fig. 5.3

When a computer is programmed with a set of statements, before any statements are executed the machine checks their legality. We have all experienced at almost every session with our microcomputers the appearance of the message 'syntax error'. As most readers will know the processor in a computer can only read and execute programs written in machine (binary) code and therefore programs written in high level languages must first be translated to such code. It is during this process of translation that, among other tasks, syntax checking takes place. As we saw from the output of Program 13, syntactically correct sentences do not necessarily convey sensible meanings. Similarly, we can have computer programs that are syntactically correct but when executed give unexpected or impossible results, or maybe will not execute at all. The translation from a high level language to machine readable code may be performed in many stages. In this text we will concern ourselves with the translation of statements from a high level language to a simplified or intermediate form of code which is capable of being interpreted by a hypothetical computer.

5.7 The language of simple expressions

To further illustrate language definition together with syntax analysis, we choose for a high level language the language of algebraic expressions.

The vocabulary (words or terminal symbols) consists of

1. the binary operators $+, -, *, /,$
2. the identifier names $A, B, C, \ldots, Z$.

An expression (sentence) is defined as follows:

1. An expression is a term or a list of terms separated by plus or minus signs.
2. A term is a primary or a list of primaries separated by multiply or divide signs.
3. A primary is a single (upper case) alphabetical character.

Using this definition we generate expressions thus:

By (1):	term	+ term
By (2):	primary * primary	+ primary
By (3):	A * B	+ C

We can see how this process is identical to that used for the fragment of English defined in Section 5.1. To formalize syntax definition for a high level programming language, a notation known as BNF (Backus Naur Form) is often used. In BNF notation the following metalinguistic symbols are used:

Symbol	Meaning
∷ −	'is a'
{ }	Items contained within braces can appear zero or more times
|	'or'
⟨ ⟩	Items contained within angle brackets are 'family' names of classes of objects (non-terminals)

Thus we can define our language of algebraic expressions as follows:

⟨expression⟩ ∷ − ⟨term⟩{⟨addop⟩⟨term⟩}
⟨term⟩   ∷ − ⟨primary⟩{⟨mulop⟩⟨primary⟩}
⟨primary⟩   ∷ − A | B | C | .... | Z
⟨addop⟩   ∷ − + | −
⟨mulop⟩   ∷ − * | /

Given the expression:

$$A + B * C + D/E$$

we produce the derivation tree given in Fig. 5.5.

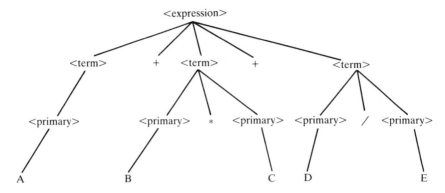

Figure 5.5 A derivation tree for the expression $A + B*C + D/E$

The proper subtrees of the derivation tree give the following phrases:

A
B
C
D
E
B * C
D/E

thus indicating the correct (unique) structure of the expression. Given the expression

$$AB + C$$

Fig. 5.6 shows an incomplete derivation tree.

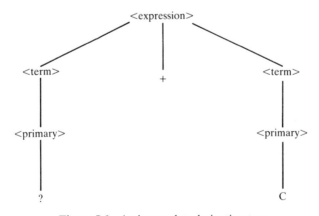

Figure 5.6 An incomplete derivation tree

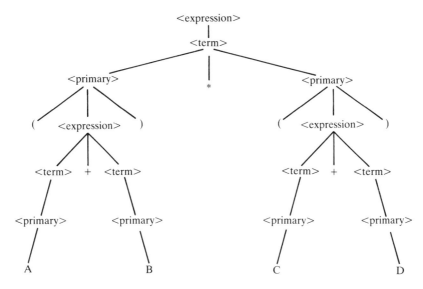

Figure 5.7 A derivation tree for the expression (A + B)*(C + D)

Our grammar for expressions does not allow the replacement of ⟨primary⟩ with AB and therefore the expression cannot be derived and is illegal.

To extend our language of expressions we allow the use of parentheses in order to override operator precedence. This requires only the rule for ⟨primary⟩ to be amended. A ⟨primary⟩ is now allowed to be a parenthesized expression as well as an alphabetic character. Thus the rule for ⟨primary⟩ becomes

⟨primary⟩ :: − A|B|C| ... |Z| (⟨expression⟩)

To illustrate the amended rule, in Fig. 5.7 we display a derivation tree for the expression

$$(A + B) * (C + D)$$

The amended grammar also allows the use of redundant parentheses in expressions.

5.8   An ambiguous grammar

Suppose we define the language of expressions by the following grammar:

⟨expression⟩ :: − A|B|C|⟨expression⟩ + ⟨expression⟩|
⟨expression⟩ − ⟨expression⟩|
⟨expression⟩ * ⟨expression⟩|
⟨expression⟩/⟨expression⟩

Given the expression A * B + C, we can draw *two* derivation trees (see Fig. 5.8).

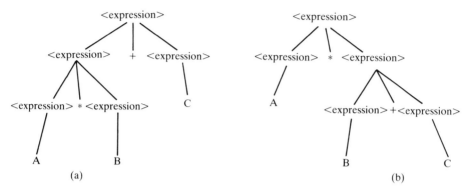

Figure 5.8 Two different derivation trees for the expression A*B+C generated by an ambiguous grammar

The phrases given by Fig. 5.8(a) are

A
B
C
A * B

while the phrases given by Fig. 5.8(b) are

A
B
C
B + C

The expression A * B + C is derived by both trees but each imply a different phrase structure. Obviously something is wrong.

The grammar does not convey a unique structural description of the expression and such a grammar is said to be *ambiguous*.

5.9   Syntax graphs

In the original description of the programming language Pascal, the syntax of the language was defined by means of *syntax graphs* instead of the usual BNF notation. The rules for drawing syntax graphs are quite straightforward and consist of:

1. For each non-terminal there is a syntax graph.
2. Each name appearing in angle brackets in BNF appears in the graph in a rectangular box.
3. All other names appear in round boxes.
4. Boxes are connected with directed lines indicating paths through the graph.

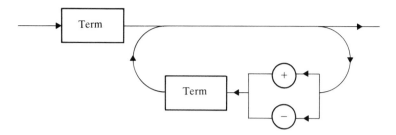

Figure 5.9   The syntax graph for expression

Applying these rules for drawing syntax graphs, we translate our BNF definition for expressions as follows:

Rule 1

$$\langle \text{expression} \rangle ::- \langle \text{term} \rangle \{ \langle \text{addop} \rangle \langle \text{term} \rangle \}$$

becomes as shown in Fig. 5.9. From observation of the graph we can see that directed paths through the graph are infinite and three examples are given:

(a) term
(b) term + term
(c) term + term − term

Rule 2

$$\langle \text{term} \rangle ::- \langle \text{primary} \rangle \{ \langle \text{mulop} \rangle \langle \text{primary} \rangle \}$$

becomes as shown in Fig. 5.10. As for expression, we see that pathways through the graph are infinite and three examples are

(a) primary
(b) primary ∗ primary
(c) primary ∗ primary/primary

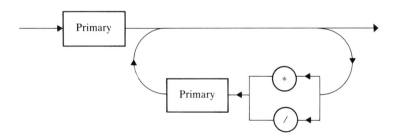

Figure 5.10   The syntax graph for term

Rule 3

$$\langle \text{primary} \rangle :: - \ A|B|C|\dots|Z|(\langle \text{expression} \rangle)$$

becomes as shown in Fig. 5.11. There are no paths in this graph which loop back on themselves and so the number of paths is finite. One of the advantages of using syntax graphs is that they provide us with flow diagrams enabling procedures to be written very easily that will analyse the syntax of a given expression.

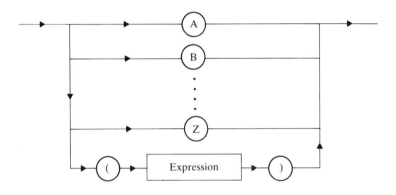

Figure 5.11   The syntax graph for primary

5.10   A syntax analyser

Using the syntax graphs as suggested we replace each graph with a procedure definition and each name in a square box with a procedure call. The pathways indicate the sequence of statements with the appropriate looping structures. Terminal symbols appearing in round boxes are just recognized and accepted (or rejected).

```
procedure EXPRESSION;
begin
  TERM;
  while sym in ['+','-']do
  begin
    GETSYM;
    TERM
  end
end;
```

```
            procedure TERM;
            begin
              PRIMARY;
              while sym in [' * ',' / ']do
              begin
                GETSYM;
                PRIMARY
              end
            end;

            procedure PRIMARY;
            begin
              if sym in ['A'. . 'Z'] then GETSYM
              else
              if sym = '('then
              begin
                GETSYM;
                EXPRESSION;
                if sym 〈 〉 ')' then ERROR else GETSYM
              end
              else
                ERROR
            end;
```

The procedure GETSYM simply reads the next symbol in the expression and assigns it to the global variable 'sym'.

5.11 Program 14

This is a program to analyse the syntax of an expression and report on its legality. Input to the program is an algebraic expression terminated by a full stop.

5.12 Expression trees

Simple expressions of the type defined in Section 5.7 can be represented by tree structures as illustrated by Fig. 5.12.

We notice that parentheses do not appear in the tree structure representation of an expression, but that their use is implied by the ordering of the tree. Thus the representation of expressions as trees does not just show nodes containing syntactic entities of the expression but also expresses the 'order of evaluation' of the expression. The expression $(A + B) * C$ is represented by the tree given in Fig. 5.13.

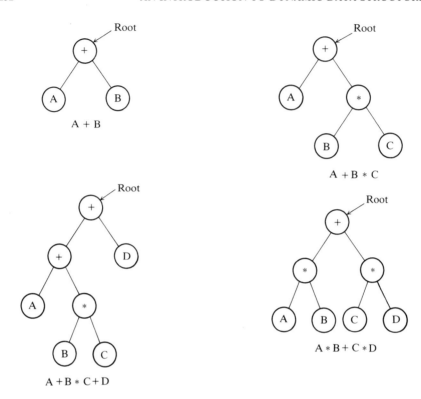

Figure 5.12   Examples of simple expression trees

The tree representing the expression $A + B * C$ given in Fig. 5.14 is quite different.

5.13   The notation of simple expressions

Expressions in mathematics and in computer science employ a number of notational devices.

Infix notation is used in the language defined in Section 5.7 and this is the most common notation used for writing expressions. In infix notation, each operator appears between its operands:

$$A * B + C$$

If we fully parenthesize the expression thus

$$((A * B) + C)$$

we see that the operands for the multiply operator are A and B while the operands for the add operator are the result of $(A * B)$ and C.

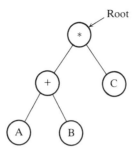

Figure 5.13   The expression tree for (A + B)∗C

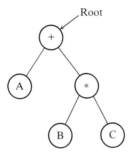

Figure 5.14   The expression tree for A + B∗C

It is possible and often useful to represent an expression using a notation other than infix. The first of these we investigate is called *prefix notation*. In this notation, each operator is followed by a parenthesized list of its operands, separated by commas. Thus the infix representation of the expression A + B would appear, in prefix notation, as

$$+(A,B)$$

Again taking the infix representation of the expression

$$A * B + C$$

and translating to its prefix form, gives

$$+(* (A,B),C)$$

A more difficult example is the expression

$$(A + B) * (C - B)$$

and this translates to the prefix notational form:

$$*(+(A,B), -(C,B))$$

The next type of notation we introduce is called *postfix notation*. This time the operator follows a parenthesized list of its operands. Using the three examples given above we show their postfix notation forms:

$$(A,B)+$$
$$((A,B)*,C)+$$
$$((A,B)+,(C,B)-)*$$

In both prefix and postfix notation (when using binary operators) we can dispense with parentheses and commas. If we now examine again the infix expression $A+B*C$, we see that because of operator precedence the sub-expression $B*C$ is evaluated first. If we wish to alter the order of evaluation so that the subexpression $A+B$ is evaluated first, we must use parentheses, thus, $(A+B)*C$. When using prefix or postfix notation, no such use of parentheses is necessary. Taking postfix as an example, the infix form $(A+B)*C$ translates to $AB+C*$, showing quite clearly that the operands of the multiply operator are the result of $A+B$ and C. These parenthesis-free forms of prefix and postfix notation are generally referred to as *polish* and *reverse polish* notation.

5.14   Traversals of expression trees

Returning to tree traversals as defined in Section 4.8 we now apply these traversals to expression trees. We take as an example the expression tree representing $A+B*C$. The order of node visitations is again indicated by the integers in Figs 5.15, 5.16 and 5.17.

We see that the in-order traversal produces the infix form of the expression (without any parentheses), while the pre-order and post-order traversals give the polish and reverse polish forms of the expression respectively.

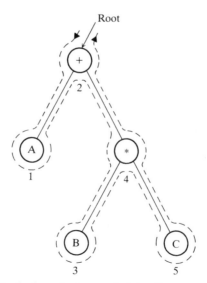

Figure 5.15   An in-order traversal giving the sequence $A+B*C$

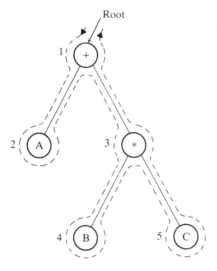

Figure 5.16 A pre-order traversal giving the sequence + A∗BC

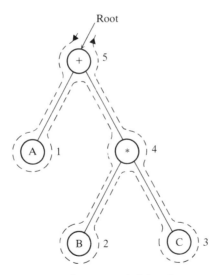

Figure 5.17 A post-order traversal giving the sequence ABC∗+

5.15 Building expression trees

As we saw in Section 5.12, the branch nodes in an expression tree contain operators and the leaf nodes contain operands. In order to design a program that will build such a tree for any expression we refer to the syntax graphs for expressions given in Section 5.9. We have already used these graphs as

EXPRESSION (tree builder)

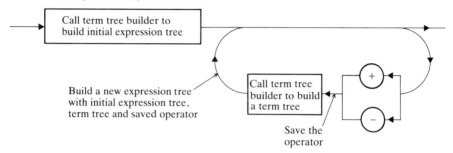

Figure 5.18   The syntax graph as a flowchart for designing a function to build an expression tree

TERM (tree builder)

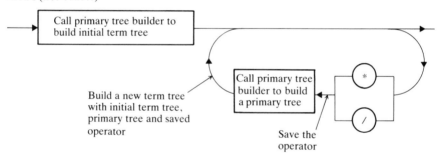

Figure 5.19   The syntax graph as a flowchart for designing a function to build a term tree

PRIMARY (tree builder)

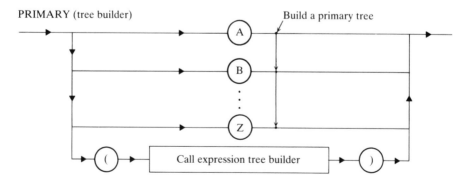

Figure 5.20   The syntax graph as a flowchart for designing a function to build a primary tree

flowcharts when designing the procedures required for syntax analysis of expressions and we now make use of flowcharts based on these graphs to design an expression tree builder program (see Figs 5.18, 5.19 and 5.20).

Each flowchart is used to design a function which returns, as value, a pointer to the tree it has built. A trace diagram showing the various function calls during building an expression tree for $A + B * C$ is given in Fig. 5.21.

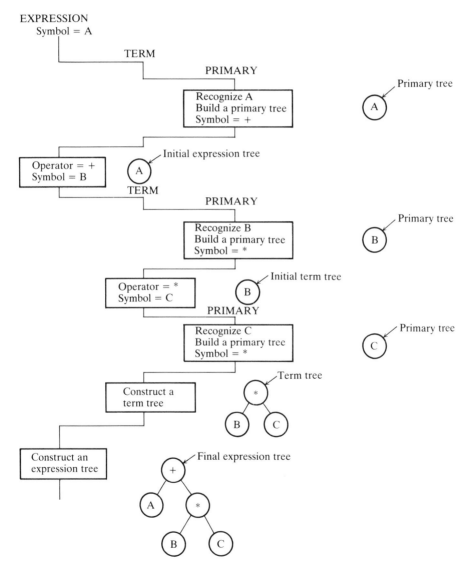

Figure 5.21 A trace diagram showing the levels of recursion encountered during a call to the expression tree builder function

The tree building functions are implemented as follows, assuming the following definitions:

```
type   tree = ↑node;
       node = record
                 op:char;
                 left,right:tree
              end;

function EXPRESSION:tree;
var t,temp:tree;
begin
  t:= TERM;
  while ch in ['+','-']do
  begin
    temp:= t;
    new(t);
    t↑.op:= sym;
    t↑.left:= temp;
    GETSYM;
    t↑.right:= TERM
  end;
  EXPRESSION:= t
end;
```

The function for building a term tree is analogous to the function just given and can be studied in the program listings. The function for building a primary tree is now given:

```
function PRIMARY:tree;
var t:tree;
begin
  if sym = '(' then
  begin
    GETSYM;
    PRIMARY:= EXPRESSION;
    if sym = ')'then GETSYM
                  else ERROR
  end
  else
  if sym in['A'..'Z']then
 ·begin
    new(t);
    t↑.op:= sym;
    t↑.left:= nil;
    t↑.right:= nil;
```

```
        GETSYM;
        PRIMARY:= t
    end
    else
    ERROR
end;
```

The procedure ERROR signals that an error has occurred in the expression and stops all tree building activities.

5.16   Program 15

Given an expression this program builds an expression tree in memory. The result of each of the three traversals (in-order, pre-order and post-order) are then printed out. The input expression must be as defined in Section 5.7 and may contain leading or embedded spaces. The expression is terminated by a full stop.

5.17   Problem set 4

1. (a) Given a binary tree representing the structure of a simple algebraic expression (i.e. as built by Program 15) write a procedure to traverse the tree and output the fully parenthesized form of the expression.
   (b) Write a procedure which reads a fully parenthesized algebraic expression from a text file and constructs its binary tree representation.
   Test these procedures in a suitable Pascal program.
2. The Dijkstra shunting yard algorithm for translating infix algebraic notation to reverse polish form is as follows. We imagine the infix expression moving in from the right in the following diagram:

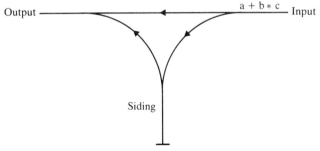

The railway siding or shunting yard

Each lexical item of the expression can either go straight across the junction or into the siding, represented by a stack, before being shunted out again. Identifiers always pass straight across to the output on the left. An incoming operator is compared for strength with the operator at the top of the siding.

If the siding operator is stronger (takes precedence over) or as strong as the incoming operator, the siding operator is popped to the output. Operators continue to be popped from the siding until the incoming operator is stronger than the operator at the top of the siding or the siding is empty; then the incoming operator goes into the siding. A left parenthesis goes straight into the siding. A right parenthesis causes operators to be popped from the siding until a left parenthesis appears; both parentheses are then discarded. The algorithm can be written more formally as follows:

```
set stack empty;
get input item;
while expression is not complete do
begin
   if input is an identifier then output it
   else
   if input is a left parenthesis then PUSH it to the stack
   else
   if input is a right parenthesis then
   begin
      POP item from stack;
      while popped item is not a left parenthesis do
      begin
         output popped item;
         POP item from stack
      end
   end
   else
   begin
      while top item is an operator and is stronger than or equal to the input
            item do
         POP item from stack to output;
      PUSH input operator to stack
   end;
get next input item
end;
while stack not empty do POP items to output;
```

Application of the algorithm to the example shown produces the following sequence of events:

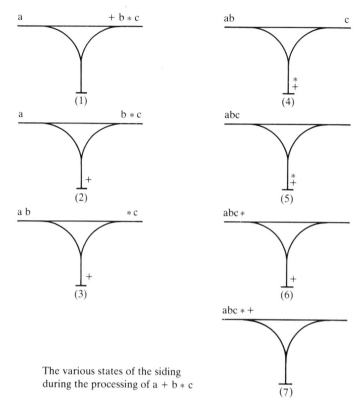

The various states of the siding
during the processing of a + b * c

Write a program to implement Dijkstra's shunting yard algorithm.

6
Evaluation of expressions

Suppose an expression is evaluated according to the following rules applied to its expression tree:

1. Evaluate the left subtree.
2. Evaluate the right subtree.
3. Apply the operator at the root.

As an example we apply these rules to the expression tree given in Fig. 6.1. As each subexpression is evaluated we show the result of evaluation in a box. Evaluation of an identifier simply means getting its value.

Obviously we cannot apply any operator until its operands have first been evaluated. Figure 6.2 shows the stages of evaluation for the expression $A + B + C * D$.

It can be seen that the nodes are visited and evaluated in the following order: $AB + CD * +$. This is in fact the reverse polish form of the expression as given by a post-order traversal (see Section 5.14 and Program 15). We saw earlier how an expression could be evaluated using two stacks; however, given the reverse polish form of an expression, we can perform the process of evaluation using only a single stack.

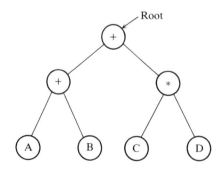

Figure 6.1   The expression tree for $A + B + C * D$

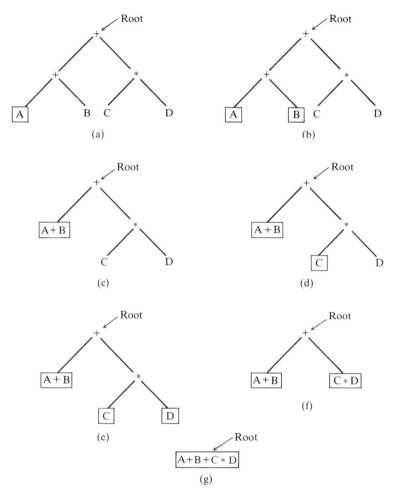

Figure 6.2 The evaluation stages of the expression represented by the tree given in Fig. 6.1

The reverse polish form of the expression is scanned from left to right and

1. if the symbol being scanned is an identifier, push its value to the stack;
2. if the symbol being scanned is an operator, apply the operator to the top two values on the stack, pop these values and push the result value of the apply operation to the stack.

A stack history during evaluation of the expression $A + B + C * D$ is given in Fig. 6.3.

If we assume the values associated with the identifiers A, B, C and D to be 1, 2, 3 and 4 respectively, the stack history is as shown in Fig. 6.4.

Stack (growing from left to right)   Expression (reverse polish form)

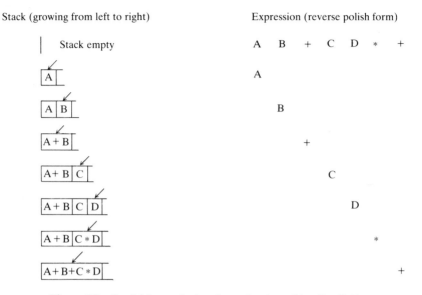

Figure 6.3   Stack history during the evaluation of A + B + C*D

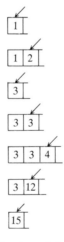

Figure 6.4   Stack history during evaluation of A + B + C*D after integer values have been assigned to A,B,C and D

6.1   Evaluation machines

The actual evaluation of an expression is performed by an evaluation machine or processor. Evaluation machines have a finite set of instructions from which must be chosen those instructions needed for the evaluation of a given expression. The task of generating these evaluation instructions is carried out by a program called a *compiler*.

We define two such evaluation machines together with the rules for generating instructions. The first of these machines is a stack-based machine. Stack evaluation of simple expressions has already been discussed and we can immediately tackle the problem of instruction generation. Stack machines require only two types of instruction:

1. a *load* instruction which pushes a value to the stack,
2. an *apply* instruction which causes an operation to be performed on elements already in the stack.

Load instructions are followed by a reference to a memory cell location from which the value to be pushed can be obtained. This memory cell reference can be, and usually is, in the form of an identifier. Apply instructions are followed by the operator, which is applied to the top two stack elements as described above. The automatic generation of these instructions is very easy as there is a one-to-one relationship between the instructions needed and the reverse polish form of the expression to be evaluated. The generation process is as follows: scan the reverse polish form of the expression and

1. if the symbol being scanned is an identifier, generate LOAD followed by the identifier name;
2. if the symbol being scanned is an operator, generate APPLY followed by the operator.

Figure 6.5 illustrates a complete process for stack machine instruction generation. Using Fig. 6.5 as a flowchart we produce the following algorithm.

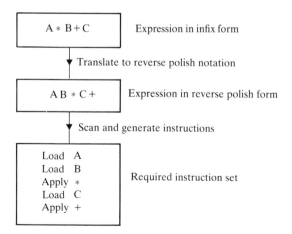

Figure 6.5   Possible stages of code generation for a stack machine

6.2   Algorithm 26. Code generation for a stack machine

```
stackcodegenerator
begin
    read expression {and possibly check for syntax errors}
    build an expression tree
    perform post-order traversal,
    scan reverse polish form obtained
    and generate instructions
end
```

The post-order tree traversal procedure already used is amended as shown to give a stack machine instruction generator.

```
procedure CODEGENERATOR(ptr:tree);
begin
    if ptr⟨ ⟩nil then
    begin
        CODEGENERATOR(ptr↑.left);
        CODEGENERATOR(ptr↑.right);
        if (ptr↑.left = nil)and(ptr↑.right = nil)then writeln('LOAD ',ptr↑.op)
                else writeln('APPLY ',ptr↑.op)
    end
end;
```

6.3   Program 16

This program, given an expression, generates code suitable for stack machine evaluation. The input expression must be as defined in Section 5.7 and may contain leading or embedded spaces. The expression is terminated by a full stop.

6.4   Code generation for a register-based machine

The second type of evaluation machine belongs to the class of register-based machines. These are the type most commonly used and rely on a special register called the *accumulator* for the evaluation of expressions. The set of available instructions is bigger than that of the stack machine and we now investigate a possible instruction set. Each instruction has two parts, an operator and an operand. An operand can be an identifier name or an actual memory cell address. Thus LOAD A is interpreted as meaning: copy the contents of the memory cell, referenced by the identifier A, to the accumulator. LOAD 12 is interpreted as meaning: copy the contents of the memory cell 12 to the accumulator. To accomplish the above interpretation there exists a table of identifier names together with their attributes. One of these attributes is an address or pointer to a memory cell. When the machine finds an identifier name

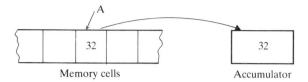

Figure 6.6   Machine state after execution of a LOAD instruction

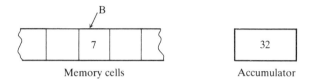

Figure 6.7   Machine state before execution of the ADD instruction

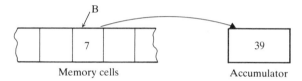

Figure 6.8   Machine state after execution of the ADD instruction

as an operand it consults this table in order to find the actual address of the memory cell referenced. Such an attribute or *symbol table* is implemented in Program 19.

If the contents of the memory cell referenced by the identifier A is the decimal number 32, LOAD A creates the machine state given in Fig. 6.6.

ADD B, MUL B, SUB B and DIV B are all interpreted as meaning: apply the operation specified using the contents of the memory cell referenced by B as its right operand and the contents of the accumulator as its left operand; the result is assigned to the accumulator, thus overwriting any existing value. For example, if the current situation is as shown in Fig. 6.7, the instruction ADD B changes the state of the machine to that given in Fig. 6.8.

It can be seen that each binary operation changes the contents of the accumulator and, unlike the stack machine, no history of its contents is available. If, therefore, at any time during the evaluation of an expression the contents of the accumulator need to be remembered, they must be copied to a safe place in memory. To facilitate this a STORE instruction is available. This instruction is interpreted as meaning: copy the contents of the accumulator to the memory cell referenced in the store instruction. Thus the instruction STORE X causes the machine to enter the state given in Fig. 6.9.

As for LOAD instructions, a STORE instruction can have an identifier name or an actual memory address as an operand.

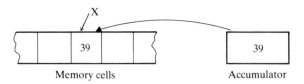

Figure 6.9   Machine state after the execution of a STORE instruction

GENERATING INSTRUCTIONS FOR AN ACCUMULATOR-TYPE MACHINE

Given the expression

$$A * B + C$$

it is fairly obvious that the instructions required are

LOAD A   (accumulator contains the value associated with the identifier A)
MUL   B   (accumulator contains the result of A * B)
ADD   C   (accumulator contains the result of A * B + C)

and that after execution of these instructions the result of evaluation is left in the accumulator.

Given the expression

$$A * B + C * D$$

we can see that after the evaluation of A * B, this result needs to be stored until C * D has been evaluated. Thus the required set of instructions is

LOAD   A
MUL   B   (accumulator contains result of A * B)
STORE 1   (save this result in memory cell 1)
LOAD   C
MUL   D   (accumulator contains result of C * D)
ADD   1   (add stored result to accumulator)

(Note that in these instructions we assume that the memory cell 1 is not referenced by any of the identifiers A, B, C or D.)

Some of the difficulties of code generation are highlighted by the following examples.

Suppose we have the expression

$$A + B * C$$

If we perform a left-to-right scan of the expression and generate instructions as the scan proceeds, the code generated is

LOAD A
ADD   B
MUL C

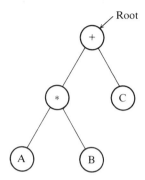

Figure 6.10 Expression tree for A*B+C

Interpreting these instructions gives an incorrect result. To obtain a correct result, the subexpression B * C must be evaluated first. Thus the correct set of instructions is

LOAD A
STORE 1
LOAD B
MUL C
ADD 1

A solution to this problem of when to generate STORE instructions can be found by careful examination of the expression tree representation of the given expression. Taking as an example the expression

$$A * B + C$$

we first construct its expression tree (see Fig. 6.10). We observe that the right subtree of each branch node (including the root) is a leaf. Thus, as we scan from left to right, the multiply operator can be applied to its operands as they are both immediately available.

We now examine the expression

$$A + B * C$$

whose expression tree is given in Fig. 6.11. When scanning from left to right the first operator we meet is the ADD operator, but we cannot apply this operator until its right operand has been evaluated (i.e. the result of B * C). Having scanned past A we cannot go back and so the value of A must be saved until it can be used.

From these observations we see that STORE instructions need to be generated when the right subtree of an operator is *not* a leaf. However, we have not yet completely solved the problem.

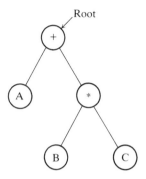

Figure 6.11   Expression tree for A + B∗C

Taking as an example the expression

$$A - B * C$$

together with the arguments just proposed, the set of instructions generated are

LOAD A
STORE 1
LOAD B
MUL   C
SUB   A

We can see that this does not reflect the meaning of the expression as we end up by subtracting A *from* the result of B ∗ C instead of subtracting the result of B ∗ C from A.

If an expression contained only the commutative operations of addition and multiplication, no further problems arise, but when the non-commutative operations of subtraction and division are involved, incorrect instructions can be generated.

The correct set of instructions for the above example is

LOAD A
STORE 1
LOAD B
MUL   C
STORE 2
LOAD 1
SUB   2

We now design a procedure that takes all these facts into consideration when generating instructions. The procedure takes as parameters an instruction and an expression tree. The next available temporary storage cell address is held in the global variable tempstore and the following definitions are assumed:

```
type  tree = ↑node;
      node = record
                  data:char;
                  left,right:tree
             end;
procedure CODEGEN(op:char;t:tree);
begin
  with t↑ do
    if data in ['A'..'Z']then
    case op of
      ' = ':writeln('LOAD ',data);
      '+':writeln('ADD ',data);
      '−':writeln('SUB ',data);
      '*':writeln('MUL ',data);
      '/ ':writeln('DIV ',data)
    end
    else
    if op = ' = ' then
    begin
      CODEGEN(' = ',left);
      CODEGEN(data,right)
    end
    else
    begin
      tempstore:= tempstore+1;
      writeln('STO t',tempstore);
      CODEGEN(' = ',left);
      CODEGEN(data,right);
      case op of
        '+':writeln('ADD t',tempstore);
        '*':writeln('MUL t',tempstore);
        '−':begin
              writeln('STO t',tempstore+1);
              writeln('LOAD t',tempstore);
              writeln('SUB t',tempstore+1)
            end;
        '/ ':begin
              writeln('STO t',tempstore+1);
              writeln('LOAD t',tempstore);
              writeln('DIV t',tempstore)
            end
      end;
      tempstore:= tempstore−1
    end
end;
```

6.5   Program 17

This is a code generator for accumulator-type evaluation machines. This program generates temporary addresses which are used for storing the value of subexpressions. These temporary addresses refer to a special section of computer memory reserved for such activities. This avoids any confusion with the section of memory referenced by identifier names. Input to the program is as described for Programs 15 and 16.

As can be seen from the listing of Program 17 the initial procedure call to generate instructions is

CODEGEN ('=',root)

and to help the reader understand the way in which this recursive procedure works we give

1. an expression tree showing the value of the parameters to the procedure at each invocation (see Fig. 6.12) and
2. a trace diagram of procedure calls (see Fig. 6.13).

6.6   Reordering of expressions

The instruction generator works on a strictly left-to-right basis and if given the expression $A + B * C$ generates the following instructions:

```
LOAD  A
STORE 1
LOAD  B
MUL   C
ADD   1
```

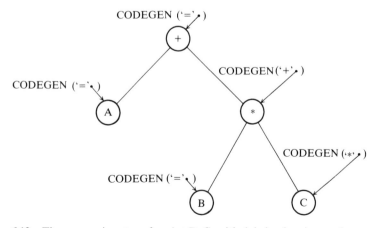

Figure 6.12   The expression tree for $A + B*C$ with labels showing code generating procedure parameters

Level   0   1   Output

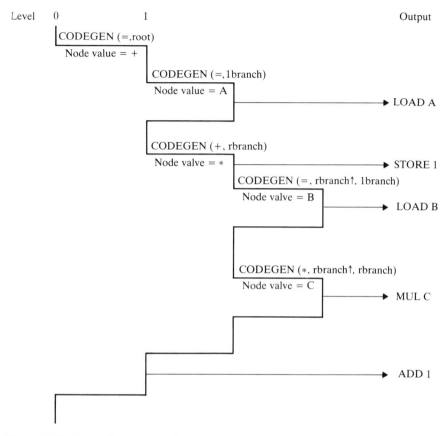

Figure 6.13   Trace diagram showing the levels of recursion encountered by calls on the code generating procedure

However, if we reordered the expression (without altering its meaning) before submitting it to the instruction generator, we could improve on the number of instructions generated.

We can reorder the expression $A + B * C$ as follows, without altering its meaning:

$$B * C + A$$

The set of instructions generated from this version of the expression is

LOAD B
MUL   C
ADD   A

giving a saving on generated instructions of 40 per cent. Figure 6.14 shows the expression trees for the initial expression and the reordered expression.

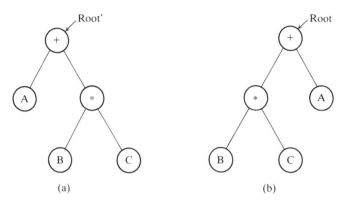

Figure 6.14   Expression trees for A + B∗C and B∗C + A

In Fig. 6.14(a) we observe the occurrence of a non-leaf right subtree whereas in Fig. 6.14(b) each right subtree is a leaf. As mentioned earlier, if all right subtrees in an expression tree are just leaves then there is no need for temporary storage (i.e. no STORE instructions are needed) as the right-hand operands of all operators are immediately available.

Thus if an expression tree can be transformed to a tree with a reduced number of non-leaf right subtrees before applying the instruction generator, the result will be a shorter, more efficient set of instructions.

6.7   Tree transformation

Transformation is not a difficult task and is easily performed by the following algorithm.

6.8   Algorithm 27. Transforming a tree

```
transformtree(ptr)
begin
   if the current node is a leaf then do nothing
   else
   begin
      if the current node contains a left subtree
         that is a leaf and a right subtree
         that is not a leaf then interchange
         subtrees.
      transformtree(lbranch(ptr))
      transformtree(rbranch(ptr))
   end
end
```

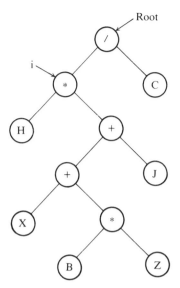

Figure 6.15 The expression tree for H*(X + B*Z + J)/C

Application of Algorithm 27 transforms any expression tree to a tree with as many right leaf subtrees as possible. We now illustrate the working of this algorithm by applying it to the expression tree representing

$$H * (X + B * Z + J)/C$$

as shown in Fig. 6.15.

The first node with a non-leaf right subtree and a leaf left subtree is the node containing the multiply operator and pointed to by 'i'. Interchanging the subtrees of this node gives the partially transformed tree shown in Fig. 6.16.

The only other node that can have its subtrees interchanged is the node pointed to by 'j' (Fig. 6.16). Interchanging the subtrees of this node gives the fully transformed tree (see Fig. 6.17).

The instructions generated by application of Program 17 to the initial expression tree given in Fig. 6.15 are

```
LOAD H
STORE 1
LOAD X
STORE 2
LOAD B
MUL   Z
ADD   2
ADD   J
MUL   1
DIV   C
```

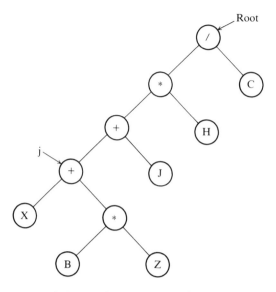

Figure 6.16   Partially transformed version of the tree given in Fig. 6.15

The instructions obtained from the transformed tree given in Fig. 6.17 are

LOAD B
MUL   Z
ADD   X
ADD   J
MUL   H
DIV   C

This latter set contains only six instructions, none of which are STORE
instructions. However, there is one further problem to solve when generating
sets of optimized instructions, and we illustrate this problem by an example. The
expression $A - B * C$ is represented by the tree given in Fig. 6.18. Applying the
transformation algorithm gives the transformed tree shown in Fig. 6.19. This
represents the reordered expression $B * C - A$.

It can be seen that the *meaning* or phrase structure of the expression has
been altered. The reordering algorithm interchanges the left and right operands
of some operators, which for commutative operations does not matter but
for non-commutative operations gives an entirely different meaning to the
expression. This problem is fairly easily rectified by introducing the concept of a
reverse operator. Any node containing a reverse operator takes its right subtree
as its left operand and its left subtree as its right operand. To help in this matter
we introduce the symbols for reverse operations as follows:

"@"   reverse subtraction
"£"   reverse division

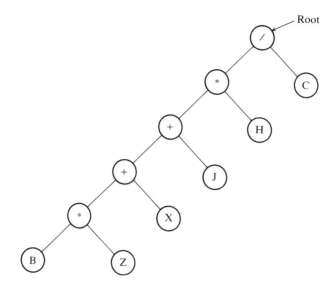

Figure 6.17 Fully transformed version of the tree given in Fig. 6.15

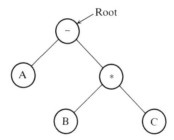

Figure 6.18 The expression tree for A − B*C

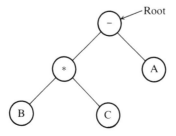

Figure 6.19 The expression tree for B*C − A

The algorithm for transforming an expression tree is now amended to take account of the reverse operators.

6.9   Algorithm 28. Use of reverse operators

```
transformtree(ptr)
begin
  if current node is a leaf then do nothing
  else
  begin
    if the right subtree of the current node
       is non-leaf
    then
    if the current node contains + or *
       and its left subtree is a leaf
       then interchange subtrees.
    if the current node contains − or /
       and its left subtree is a leaf
       then interchange subtrees and
       reverse the operator at the current node.
    transformtree(left subtree)
    transformtree(right subtree)
  end
end
```

Algorithm 28 is implemented by the following procedures:

```
procedure TRANSFORMTREE(ptr:tree);
  procedure SWAP;
  var temp:tree;
  begin
    temp:= ptr↑.left;
    ptr↑.left:= ptr↑.right;
    ptr↑.right:= temp
  end;
  begin
  with ptr↑ do
    if data in ['+','−','*','/ ']then
    begin
      if right↑.data in['+','−','*','/ ']then
      case data of
        '+','*':if left↑.data in['A'..'Z']then SWAP;
        '−':begin
              SWAP;
              data:= '@'
            end;
```

```
  ' / ':begin
           SWAP;
           data : = '£'
        end
     end;
     TRANSFORMTREE(left);
     TRANSFORMTREE(right)
  end
end;
```

Given the transformed tree for the expression $A - B * C$ shown in Fig. 6.19 and if we now apply the code generating procedure of Program 17 we get the following set of instructions:

```
LOAD B
MUL  C
RSUB A
```

We could leave the instruction set in this form and assume that the meaning of reverse operations is understood by the evaluation machine. Alternatively, we could amend the code generating procedure to make sure that no reverse operators appear in the final set of instructions. In Program 18 we choose this alternative. Thus given the tree in Fig. 6.19, Program 18 generates the following code:

```
LOAD  B
MUL   C
STORE 1
LOAD  A
SUB   1
```

6.10   Program 18

This program generates optimized code for an accumulator-type machine. Input to the program is an algebraic expression as defined for Program 17. A tree representing the expression is built in memory. This is then used to generate a listing of the code required for expression evaluation. A transformed tree is then built and the optimized code obtained from this tree is listed as output. The reader should note the use of reverse operators in the transformed trees, but, as mentioned in the text, these do not appear in the generated code.

7
A complete expression evaluation system

We now bring together some of the tree operations discussed in the text in order to illustrate their possible application in the design of a simple expression evaluation system. The system accepts two types of statements:

1. Declaration of constants
2. Expressions involving declared constants

Constant declaration statements *must* precede expression statements. Declarations are stored by the system and expressions are evaluated by the system. A set of declaration and expression statements is called a *program*. For example,

$$A = 12, B = 14;$$
$$A + B;$$
$$A + B - B;$$
$$A + B + B * A;$$
$$A - B * C.$$

As can be seen, individual declaration statements are separated by commas and complete declaration and expression statements by semi-colons; the program is

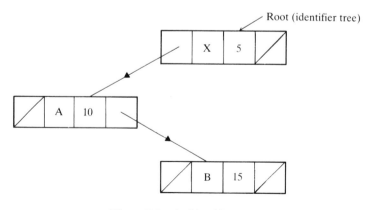

Figure 7.1 An identifier tree

terminated by a full stop. In declaration statements, constants can only be assigned integer values and expressions are evaluated using integer arithmetic.

We can design such a system in at least two ways:

1. as an *interpretive* system or
2. as a *compiled* system.

7.1   The interpretive system

As identifiers are declared they are stored together with their associated values in an identifier tree. Figure 7.1 shows the identifier tree after the following sample declarations have been made:

$$X = 5, A = 10, B = 15;$$

It should be noted that the identifier tree is constructed as a binary search tree.

Thus, when expressions are being analysed and evaluated, the identifier tree can be searched to see if identifiers exist and if so then their values obtained. Expressions are evaluated by the 'tree pruning' process as described in Chapter 6; i.e. given

$$A = 3, B = 15;$$

the evaluation of $A + B$ proceeds as follows:

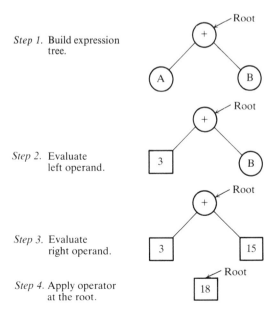

Step 1. Build expression tree.

Step 2. Evaluate left operand.

Step 3. Evaluate right operand.

Step 4. Apply operator at the root.

An overall view of the system is given in Fig. 7.2.

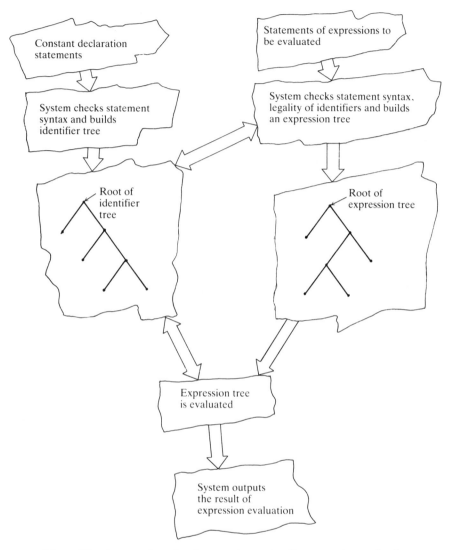

Figure 7.2 An overview of an interpretive system for expression evaluation

7.2 Program 19

This is a complete interpretive evaluation system. Input to the system is a 'program' as defined at the beginning of the chapter. In the case of an expression containing an error the error procedure signals this fact and also prints out an error code in order to give some indication of the type of error. This is a simple form of error checking but is an improvement on earlier programs. In order to keep the system as simple as possible, once an error has been discovered the complete 'program' needs to be re-entered. The following are the error codes used:

1. Identifier twice declared
2. Illegal identifier name
3. 'Equals' sign expected
4. Identifier used in expression has not been declared
5. Missing right parenthesis
6. Illegal symbol in expression

7.3 The compiled system

By examination of the system outline given in Fig. 7.3 it can be seen that the front end of this system is the same as that just described for the interpretive system.

However, after the expression tree has been created it is then used to generate machine code which in turn is executed by an interpreter. In the system given we have chosen to generate code suitable for a stack machine. As code is generated it has to be stored in memory ready for execution. To model this code store we use a linked list of records, assuming the following definitions:

$$\text{type iptr} = \uparrow\text{inode};$$
$$\text{inode} = \text{record}$$
$$\text{op,oprand:char};$$
$$\text{next:iptr}$$
$$\text{end};$$

Each operator will be stored as 'L' or 'A'.

The system could just as easily be made to produce code for a one-address or accumulator type of machine. The only part of this system not covered in earlier sections of the text is the interpreter, which executes the generated code. The interpreter simply simulates a stack machine that has the following instruction set, which can be studied in more detail in Program 20:

LOAD ⟨identifier⟩
APPLY ⟨operator⟩
STOP

The LOAD instruction pushes the value associated with the given identifier to the stack. The APPLY instruction pops the top two stack elements and applies the operator to them, pushing the resulting value back to the stack. When the end of the generated code is reached the result of the expression evaluation is found on top of the stack. This is then printed out and removed from the stack.

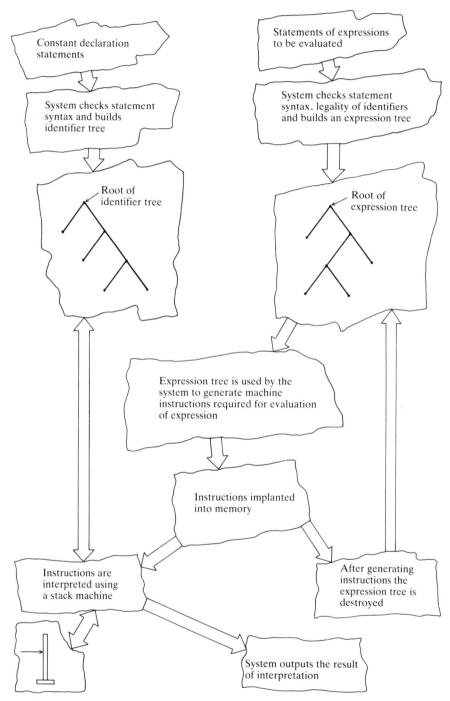

Figure 7.3   An overview of a compiler/interpreter system for expression evaluation

To model the stack we again use a linked list of records, the type definitions being as follows:

```
type sptr = ↑snode;
     snode = record
                   data:integer;
                   next:sptr
             end;
```

A variable called *stackpointer* always points to the top stack element.

7.4 Program 20

This is a complete microcompiler system. Input to the system is as defined for Program 19 and the system performs the following tasks:

1. The analysis of statements
2. The storing of information about constants
3. The generation of instructions needed for evaluation of expressions

The above processes are generally referred to as *compilation*. Finally, the generated instructions are listed and then executed on a stack-type evaluation machine. Programs 19 and 20 represent relatively simple systems but can provide the basis for much more complex and powerful systems.

PART THREE

Partial listings

Program 1

```
program one(input,output);
type link = ^node;
   node = record
             data:char;
             next:link
          end;
var listhead:link;
procedure BUILDALISTINREVERSE(var ptr:link);
    ⋮

procedure WRITEALIST(ptr:link);
    ⋮

begin {main program}
   BUILDALISTINREVERSE(listhead);
   WRITELIST(listhead)
end.
```

Program 2

```
program two(input,output);
type link = ^node;
     node = record
              data:char;
              next:link
            end;
var listhead:link;
    ch:char;
procedure BUILDALISTINREVERSE(var ptr:link);
       .
       .
procedure SEARCHLIST(ptr:link;item:char);
       .
       .
begin {main program}
  BUILDALISTINREVERSE(listhead);
  writeln('Input item to search for');
  readln(ch);
  SEARCHLIST(listhead,ch)
end.
```

Program 3

```
program three(input,output);
type link = ^node;
    node = record
                data:char;
                next:link
            end;
var listhead,endptr:link;
    ch:char;
    choice:integer;
procedure SEARCHLIST(ptr:link;item:char);
            :
procedure SEARCHANDINSERT(var ptr:link;item:char);
            :
procedure SEARCHANDDELETE(var ptr:link;item:char);
            :
procedure WRITEALIST(ptr:link);
            :
procedure BUILDORDEREDLIST(var ptr:link);
            :
procedure MENU;
var i:integer;
begin
    for i:= 1 to 25 do writeln;
    writeln('1:Buildalist');
    writeln('2:Write list contents');
    writeln('3:Delete a node');
    writeln('4:Insert a node');
    writeln('5:Search list');
    writeln('6:Finished');
    readln(choice)
end;
```

```
begin {main program}
  MENU;
  while choice⟨ ⟩6 do
  begin
    case choice of
    1:BUILDORDEREDLIST(listhead);
    2:begin
        WRITELIST(listhead);
        writeln('Press a key to continue');
        get(input)
      end;
    3:begin
        writeln('Please input item to delete');
        readln(ch);
        SEARCHANDDELETE(listhead,ch)
      end;
    4:begin
        writeln('Item to be inserted');
        readln(ch);
        SEARCHANDINSERT(listhead,ch);
      end;
    5:begin
        writeln('Item to search for');
        readln(ch);
        SEARCHLIST(listhead,ch);
        writeln('Press a key to continue');
        get(input)
      end;
    end;
    MENU
  end;
  writeln('Program finished')
end.
```

Program 4

```
program four(input,output);
type link = ^person;
     person = record
                   ctype:char;
                   next:link
               end;
var queuehead,endqueue,temp:link;
    clock,barberfree,queuelength,servicetime,rn:integer;

function RANDOM:real;
        ⋮

procedure JOINQUEUE;
        ⋮

procedure SERVICECUSTOMER;
        ⋮

procedure BARBERSHOP;
        ⋮

begin {main program}
   writeln('Input random number seed');
   readln(rn);
   BARBERSHOP
end.
```

Program 5

```
program five(input,output);
type link = ^node;
   node = record
              data:integer;
              next:link
           end;
var stackheadptr,temp:link;
   number,base:integer;

procedure PUSH(var ptr:link;var item:integer);
   :

procedure PRINTSTACK(ptr:link); {same as WRITEALIST}
   :

procedure CHANGENUMBERBASE;
   :

begin {main program}
   CHANGENUMBERBASE
end.
```

Program 6

```
program six(input,output);
type symbol = (add,sub,dov,mul,stop,value,lparen,rparen);
 olink = ^onode;
 vlink = ^vnode;
onode = record
          data:char;
          next:olink
        end;
vnode = record
          data:integer;
          next:vlink
        end;
var op,ch:char;
    otop:olink;
    vtop:vlink;
    sym:symbol;
    num,lop,rop,res:integer;
    finished:boolean;

procedure PUSHVAL(item:integer);
var temp:vlink;
begin
  new(temp);
  temp^.data := item;
  temp^.next := vtop;
  vtop := temp
end;

procedure POPVAL(var item:integer);
begin
  item := vtop^.data;
  vtop := vtop^.next
end;
```

```
procedure PUSHOP(item:char);
var temp:olink;
begin
  new(temp);
  temp^.data:= item;
  temp^.next:= otop;
  otop:= temp
end;

procedure POPOP(var item:char);
begin
  item:= otop^.data;
  otop:= otop^.next
end;

procedure EXECUTE;
begin
  POPVAL(rop);
  POPVAL(lop);
  case op of
  '+':res:= lop+rop;
  '-':res:= lop-rop;
  '*':res:= lop*rop;
  '/ ':res:= lop DIV rop
  end;
  PUSHVAL(res)
end;

function STRENGTH(op:char):integer;
begin
  case op of
  ' (',' ) ':STRENGTH:= 0;
  '+','-':STRENGTH:= 1;
  '*','/ ':STRENGTH:= 2
  end
end;
```

```
procedure GETSYM;
begin
  while input^ = ' 'do get(input);
  if input^ in ['0'..'9'] then
  begin
    sym := value;
    num := 0;
    repeat
      num := 10 * num + ord(input)^ − ord('0');
      get(input)
    until not(input^ in['0'..'9'])
  end
  else
  begin
    case input^ of
    '+':sym := add;
    '−':sym := sub;
    '*':sym := mul;
    '/':sym := dov;
    '(':sym := lparen;
    ')':sym := rparen;
    '.':sym := stop
    end;
    ch := input^;
    get(input)
  end
end;

begin {main program}
  otop := nil;
  vtop := nil;
  finished := false;
  GETSYM;
  while sym < > stop do
  begin
    if sym = value then PUSHVAL(num)
    else
    if(otop = nil)or(sym = lparen)then PUSHOP(ch)
    else
    if sym = rparen then
```

```
    begin
      POPOP(op);
      while op ⟨⟩ '(' do
      begin
        EXECUTE;
        POPOP(op)
      end
    end
    else
    if STRENGTH(ch) > STRENGTH(otop^.data)then PUSHOP(ch)
    else
    begin
      while not finished do
      begin
        if STRENGTH(otop^.data) > = STRENGTH(ch)then
        begin
          POPOP(op);
          EXECUTE
        end
        else
        finished: = true;
        if otop = nil then finished: = true
      end;
      PUSHOP(ch)
    end;
    GETSYM;
    finished: = false
  end;
  while otop⟨ ⟩nil do
  begin
    POPOP(op);
    EXECUTE
  end;
  writeln('Result is ',vtop^.data)
end.
```

Program 7

```
program seven(input,output);
type link = ^node;
     node = record
               data:integer;
               next:link
            end;
var set1,set2:link;
        num:integer;
function HEAD(ptr:link):integer;
   :
function TAIL(ptr:link):link;
   :
function PREFIX(item:integer;ptr:link):link;
   :
function REVERSE(ptr:link):link;
   :
procedure WRITEALIST(ptr:link);
   :
function INTERSECTION(ptr1,ptr2:link):link;
   :
function UNION(ptr1,ptr2:link):link;
   :
function ISANELEMENTOF(ptr:link;item:integer):boolean;
   :
function EQUALSETS(ptr1,ptr2:link):boolean;
   :
function SUBSET(ptr1,ptr2:link):boolean;
   :
function DIFFERENCE(ptr1,ptr2:link):link;
   :
```

```
function BUILDALIST:link;
var list:link;
    num:integer;
begin
  list:= nil;
  readln(num);
  while num > 0 do
  begin
    list:= PREFIX(num,list);
    readln(num)
  end;
  BUILDALIST:= list
end;

begin {main program}
  set1:= nil;
  set2:= nil;
  set1:= BUILDALIST;
  set1:= REVERSE(set1);
  writeln('Set1');
  writeln;
  WRITELIST(set1);
  set2:= BUILDALIST;
  set2:= REVERSE(set2);
  writeln('Set2');
  writeln;
  WRITELIST(set2);
  writeln('The union is');
  WRITELIST(UNION(set1,set2));
  writeln;
  writeln('The intersection is');
  WRITELIST(INTERSECTION(set1,set2));
  writeln;
  writeln('Input number to test for membership');
  writeln('of set1');
  readln(num);
  writeln(ISANELEMENTOF(set1,num));
  writeln;
  writeln('The difference is');
  WRITELIST(DIFFERENCE(set1,set2));
  writeln;
  writeln('Testing for equality');
  writeln(EQUALSETS(set1,set2))
end.
```

Program 8

```
program eight(input,output);
type aptr = ^anode;
     bptr = ^bnode;
     string = packed array[1..20]of char;
     anode = record
                  name:string;
                  head,endp:bptr;
                  next:aptr
             end;
     bnode = record
                  title:string;
                  next:bptr
             end;

var library,authorptr,endptr:aptr;
    choice:integer;
    name,title:string;
    found:boolean;

procedure WAIT;
var c:char;
begin
  writeln('Press key c to continue');
  readln(c)
end;
```

```
procedure READSTRING(var n:string);
var i:integer;
    ch:char;
begin
  for i:= 1 to 20 do n[i]:= ' ';
  i:= 1;
  while not eoln do
  begin
    read(ch);
    n[i]:= ch;
    i:= i+1
  end;
  readln
end;

procedure CLEAR;
var i:integer;
begin
  for i:= 1 to 25 do writeln
end;

procedure INSERTAUTHOR(var ptr:aptr;n:string);
var temp,search:aptr;
    inserted:boolean;
begin
  new(temp);
  temp^.name:= n;
  temp^.next:= nil;
  temp^.head:= nil;
  temp^.endp:= nil;
  inserted:= false;
  search:= ptr;
  if ptr = nil then
  begin
    ptr:= temp;
    endptr:= temp
  end
  else
  if n < ptr^.name then
  begin
    temp^.next:= ptr;
    ptr:= temp
  end
  else
  if n > endptr^.name then
```

```
begin
  endptr^.next := temp;
  endptr := temp
end
else
repeat
  if(n > = search^.name)and(n < search^.next^.name)then
  begin
    temp^.next := search^.next;
    search^.next := temp;
    inserted := true
  end
  else
  search := search^.next
until inserted
end;

procedure DELETEAUTHOR(var ptr:aptr;n:string);
var search1,search2:aptr;
begin
  search1 := ptr;
  if search1 = nil then writeln('Empty library')
  else
  if search1^.name = n then ptr := search1^.next
  else
  begin
    while(search1^.next< >nil)and(search1^.name< >n)do
    begin
      search2 := search1;
      search1 := search1^.next
    end;
    if search1^.name = n then
    begin
      search2^.next := search1^.next;
      if search1 = endptr then endptr := search2
    end
    else
    writeln('Author not in library')
  end
end;
```

```
procedure SEARCHFORAUTHOR(ptr:aptr;n:string);
begin
  if ptr = nil then
  begin
    writeln('Author not found');
    found: = false
  end
  else
  if n = ptr^.name then
  begin
    found: = true;
    authorptr: = ptr
  end
  else
  SEARCHFORAUTHOR(ptr^.next,n)
end;

procedure INSERTBOOK(var ptr:aptr;t:string);
var temp,search:bptr;
    inserted:boolean;
begin
  new(temp);
  temp^.title: = t;
  temp^.next: = nil;
  search: = ptr^.head;
  inserted: = false;
  if ptr^.head = nil then
  begin
    ptr^.head: = temp;
    ptr^.endp: = temp
  end
  else
  if t < ptr^.head^.title then
  begin
    temp^.next: = ptr^.head;
    ptr^.head: = temp
  end
  else
  if t > ptr^.endp^.title then
  begin
    ptr^.endp^.next: = temp;
    ptr^.endp: = temp
  end
  else
```

```pascal
    repeat
      if (t > = search^.title)and(t < search^.next^.title)then
      begin
        temp^.next:= search^.next;
        search^.next:= temp;
        inserted:= true
      end
      else
      search:= search^.next
    until inserted
end;

procedure DELETEBOOK(var ptr:aptr;t:string);
var search1,search2:bptr;
begin
  search1:= ptr^.head;
  if search1 = nil then writeln('No books by this author')
  else
  if search1^.title = t then ptr^.head:= search1^.next
  else
  begin
  while(search^.next< >nil)and(search1^.title< >t)do
  begin
    search2:= search1;
    search1:= search1^.next
  end;
  if search1^.title = t then
  begin
    search2^.next:= search1^.next;
    if search1 = ptr^.endp then ptr^.endp:= search2
  end
  else
  writeln('Book not in list')
  end
end;

procedure WRITEBOOKS(ptr:aptr;t:integer);
var book:bptr;
begin
  book:= ptr^.head;
  while book< >nil do
  begin
    writeln(book^.title:t);
    book:= book^.next
  end
end;
```

```
procedure WRITEAUTHORS(ptr:aptr);
begin
  while ptr⟨ ⟩nil do
  begin
    writeln(ptr^.name);
    ptr := ptr^.next
  end
end;

procedure WRITELIBRARY(ptr:aptr);
var book:bptr;
begin
  while ptr⟨ ⟩nil do
  begin
    writeln(ptr^.name:20);
    WRITEBOOKS(ptr,30);
    ptr := ptr^.next
  end
end;

procedure MENU;
begin
  CLEAR;
  writeln('Choose option by number');
  writeln;writeln;
  writeln('1:New author');
  writeln('2:Delete author');
  writeln('3:Add books to existing author');
  writeln('4:Delete books by existing author');
  writeln('5:Print out complete library');
  writeln('6:Print out author list');
  writeln('7:Print out titles by a given author');
  writeln('8:Finished');
  repeat
    readln(choice)
  until (choice > = 1)and(choice < = 8)
end;
```

```
procedure OPTIONS;
begin
  case choice of
  1:begin
      CLEAR;
      writeln('Input new author');
      READSTRING(name);
      INSERTAUTHOR(library,name)
    end;
  2:begin
      CLEAR;
      writeln('Input author to be deleted');
      READSTRING(name);
      DELETEAUTHOR(library,name)
    end;
  3:begin
      CLEAR;
      writeln('Input author name');
      READSTRING(name);
      SEARCHFORAUTHOR(library,name);
      if found then
      begin
        writeln('Input new title');
        READSTRING(title);
        INSERTBOOK(authorptr,title)
      end
    end;
  4:begin
      CLEAR;
      writeln('Input author');
      READSTRING(name);
      SEARCHFORAUTHOR(library,name);
      if found then
      begin
        writeln('Input title to be deleted');
        READSTRING(title);
        DELETEBOOK(authorptr,title)
      end
    end;
  5:begin
      CLEAR;
      WRITELIBRARY(library)
    end;
```

```
    6:begin
        CLEAR;
        WRITEAUTHORS(library)
      end;
    7:begin
        CLEAR;
        writeln('Input author name');
        READSTRING(name);
        SEARCHFORAUTHOR(library,name);
        if found then
        begin
          CLEAR;
          WRITEBOOKS(authorptr,20)
        end
      end;
    8:begin
        CLEAR;
        writeln('Finished')
      end
    end;
    WAIT
end;

begin {main program}
  library:= nil;
  endptr:= nil;
  repeat
    MENU;
    OPTIONS
  until choice = 8
end.
```

Program 9

```
program nine(input,output);
type link = ^node;
  node = record
    data:char;
    lbranch,rbranch:link
  end;
var root:link;
  item:char;

procedure GROWALEAF(var ptr:link;i:char);
        ⋮

procedure BUILDBINARYSEARCHTREE;
        ⋮

begin {main program}
  BUILDBINARYSEARCHTREE
end.
```

Program 10

```pascal
program ten(input,output);
type link = ^node;
    node = record
                data:char;
                lbranch,rbranch:link
            end;
var root:link;
item:char;
choice:integer;

procedure WAIT;
var c:char;
begin
  writeln('press any key');
  readln(c)
end;

procedure CLEAR;
var i:integer;
begin
  for i:= 1 to 25 do writeln
end;

procedure GROWALEAF(var ptr:link;i:char);
        ⋮

procedure BUILDBINARYSEARCHTREE;
        ⋮

procedure INORDER(ptr:link);
        ⋮

procedure PREORDER(ptr:link);
        ⋮

procedure POSTORDER(ptr:link);
        ⋮
```

```
procedure INSERTLEAF(var ptr:link;i:char);
      ⋮

procedure FINDANDDELETE(var ptr:link;item:char);
      ⋮

procedure MENU;
begin
  CLEAR;
  writeln('Choose option by number');
  writeln;writeln;
  writeln('1:Build a Binary Search Tree);
  writeln('2:Tree traversals');
  writeln('3:Insert a new node');
  writeln('4:Delete a node');
  writeln('5:Finished');
  repeat
    readln(choice)
  until(choice > = )and(choice < = 5)
end;
```

```
procedure OPTIONS;
begin
  case choice of
  1:BUILDBINARYSEARCHTREE;
  2:begin
      CLEAR;
      writeln('Preorder traversal');
      PREORDER(root);
      writeln;writeln;
      writeln('Inorder traversal');
      INORDER(root);
      writeln;writeln;
      writeln('Postorder traversal');
      POSTORDER(root);
      writeln;writeln
    end;
  3:begin
      CLEAR;
      writeln('Input item to be inserted');
      readln(item);
      INSERTLEAF(root,item) {or GROWALEAF}
    end;
  4:begin
      CLEAR;
      writeln('Input item to be deleted');
      readln(item);
      FINDANDDELETE(root,item)
    end;
  5:writeln('Program finished')
  end;
  WAIT
end;

begin {main program}
  repeat
    MENU;
    OPTIONS
  until choice = 5
end.
```

Program 11

```
program eleven(input,output);
type link1 = ^vnode;
     link2 = ^anode;
     vnode = record
                 vernum,edgesin:integer;
                 nextv:link1;
                 adjlist:link2
             end;
     anode = record
                 vernum:integer;
                 nexta:link2
             end;
var graph,index,ivertex,newvertex:link1;
    ver1,ver2,nov:integer;
    newadj:link2;

procedure SEARCHFORVERTEX(ptr:link1;vnum:integer);
    ⋮

procedure UPDATEVERTEX(ptr:link1;vnum:integer);
    ⋮
```

```
procedure BUILDGRAPH;
var i:integer;
begin
  graph := nil;
  writeln('How many vertices?');
  readln(nov);
  for i := nov downto 1 do
  begin
    new(newvertex);
    newvertex^.vernum := i;
    newvertex^.nextv := graph;
    newvertex^.edgesin := 0;
    newvertex^.adjlist := nil;
    graph := newvertex
  end;
  writeln('Input ordered pairs');
  readln(ver1,ver2);
  repeat
    SEARCHFORVERTEX(graph,ver1);
    UPDATEVERTEX(index,ver2);
    SEARCHFORVERTEX(graph,ver2);
    index^.edgesin := index^.edgesin + 1;
    writeln('Next ordered pair');
    readln(ver1,ver2)
  until(ver1 = 0)and(ver2 = 0)
end;
```

```
procedure DELVERTEX(ptr1,ptr2:link1);
var deleted:boolean;
begin
  if ptr1 = ptr2 then graph:= ptr1^.nextv
  else
  begin
    deleted:= false;
    repeat
      if ptr1^.nextv = ptr2 then
      begin
        if ptr1^.nextv^.nextv = nil then
        begin
          ptr1^.nextv:= nil;
          deleted:= true
        end
        else
        begin
          ptr1^.nextv:= ptr1^.nextv^.nextv;
          deleted:= true
        end
      end
      else
      ptr1:= ptr1^.nextv
    until deleted
  end
end;

procedure REMEDGES(ptr:link2);
begin
  if ptr⟨ ⟩nil then
  begin
    SEARCHFORVERTEX(graph,ptr^.vernum);
    index^.edgesin:= index^.edgesin − 1;
    REMEDGES(ptr^.nexta)
  end
end;

procedure SEARCHZEROCOUNT(ptr:link1;num:integer);
begin
  if ptr⟨ ⟩nil then
  if ptr^.edgesin = num then
  index:= ptr
  else
  SEARCHZEROCOUNT(ptr ^.nextv,num)
end;
```

```
procedure TOPOLSORT;
var tab:integer;
begin
  tab:= 2;
  repeat
    SEARCHZEROCOUNT(graph,0);
    ivertex:= index;
    REMEDGES(ivertex^.adjlist);
    write(ivertex^.vernum:tab);
    DELVERTEX(graph,ivertex)
  until graph = nil
end;

begin {main program}
  BUILDGRAPH;
  TOPOLSORT
end.
```

Program 12

```
program twelve(input,output);
type link1 = ^vnode;
     link2 = ^anode;
     link = ^snode;
     vnode = record
                  vernum,weight:integer;
                  nextv:link1;
                  adjlist,endp:link2
              end;
     anode = record
                  vernum,weight,flag:integer;
                  nexta:link2
              end;
     snode = record
                  value:link1;
                  length:integer;
                  next:link
              end;
var graph,index,ivertex,newvertex:link1;
    ver1,ver2,nov,wf,sopv:integer;
    newadj,aindex:link2;
    stackpointer,rsp:link;
```

```
procedure FIXENDPTS(ptr:link1);
var search:link2;
begin
  while ptr⟨ ⟩nil do
  begin
    search := ptr^.adjlist;
    if search⟨ ⟩nil then
    begin
      while search^.nexta⟨ ⟩nil do search := search^.nexta;
    end;
    ptr^.endp := search;
    ptr := ptr^.nextv
  end
end;

procedure SEARCHFORVERTEX(ptr:link1;vnum:integer);
begin
  if ptr⟨ ⟩nil then
  if ptr^.vernum = vnum then index := ptr
  else
  SEARCHFORVERTEX(ptr^.nextv,vnum)
end;

procedure UPDATEVERTEX(ptr:link1;vnum,wt:integer);
begin
  new(newadj);
  newadj^.vernum := vnum;
  newadj^.weight := wt;
  newadj^.flag := 0;
  newadj^.nexta := ptr^.adjlist;
  ptr^.adjlist := newadj
end;
```

```
procedure BUILDGRAPH;
var i:integer;
begin
  graph:= nil;
  writeln('How many vertices?');
  readln(nov);
  for i:= nov downto 1 do
  begin
    new(newvertex);
    newvertex^.vernum:= i;
    newvertex^.nextv:= graph;
    newvertex^.adjlist:= nil;
    newvertex^.endp:= nil;
    graph:= newvertex
  end;
  writeln('Input ordered pairs');
  readln(ver1,ver2);
  repeat
    writeln('Weight Factor ?');
    readln(wf);
    SEARCHFORVERTEX(graph,ver1);
    UPDATEVERTEX(index,ver2,wf);
    writeln('Next ordered pair');
    readln(ver1,ver2)
  until(ver1 = 0)and(ver2 = 0);
  FIXENDPTS(graph)
end;

procedure PUSH(ptr:link1;length:integer);
var newsnode:link;
begin
  new(newsnode);
  newsnode^.value:= ptr;
  newsnode^.length:= length;
  newsnode^.next:= stackpointer;
  stackpointer:= newsnode
end;

procedure POP;
begin
  stackpointer:= stackpointer^.next
end;
```

```
procedure ZEROFLAGS(ptr:link2);
begin
  if ptr⟨ ⟩nil then
  begin
    ptr^.flag:= 0;
    ZEROFLAGS(ptr^.nexta)
  end
end;

function LENGTHOFPATH(ptr:link):integer;
var total:integer;
begin
  total:= 0;
  while ptr⟨ ⟩nil do
  begin
    total:= total + ptr^.length;
    ptr:= ptr^.next
  end;
  LENGTHOFPATH:= total
end;

procedure PRINTSTACK(ptr:link);
begin
  while ptr⟨ ⟩nil do
  begin
    write(ptr^.value^.vernum:3);
    ptr:= ptr^.next;
    if ptr⟨ ⟩nil then write('− >')
  end;
  writeln('Pathlength = ',LENGTHOFPATH(stackpointer):5)
end;

procedure REVERSESTACK(ptr:link);
var newsnode:link;
begin
  rsp:= nil;
  repeat
    new(newsnode);
    newsnode^.value:= ptr^.value;
    newsnode^.next:= rsp;
    rsp:= newsnode;
    ptr:= ptr^.next
  until ptr = nil
end;
```

```
procedure FINDALLPATHS;
begin
  stackpointer: = nil;
  writeln('Enter start vertex');
  readln(sopv);
  SEARCHFORVERTEX(graph,sopv);
  if (index^.adjlist = nil)or(nov = 1)then writeln('No paths from this vertex')
  else
  begin
    PUSH(index,0);
    while index^.adjlist⟨ ⟩nil do
    begin
      aindex: = index^.adjlist;
      aindex^.flag: = 1;
      SEARCHFORVERTEX(graph,aindex^.vernum);
      PUSH(index,aindex^.weight)
    end;
    REVERSESTACK(stackpointer);
    PRINTSTACK(rsp);
    POP;
    while stackpointer⟨ ⟩nil do
    begin
      index: = stackpointer^.value;
      aindex: = stackpointer^.value^.adjlist;
      while( aindex^.flag = 1)and(aindex⟨ ⟩stackpointer^.value^.endp) do
        if aindex^.flag = 1 then aindex: = aindex^.nexta;
        if( aindex^.flag = 1)and(aindex = stackpointer^.value^.endp) then
        begin
          ZEROFLAGS(stackpointer^.value^.adjlist);
          POP
        end
        else
        begin
          aindex^.flag: = 1;
          SEARCHFORVERTEX(graph,aindex^.vernum);
          PUSH(index,aindex^.weight);
          while index^.adjlist⟨ ⟩nil do
          begin
            aindex: = index^.adjlist;
            aindex^.flag: = 1;
            SEARCHFORVERTEX(graph,aindex^.vernum);
            PUSH(index,aindex^.weight)
          end;
```

```
            REVERSESTACK(stackpointer);
            PRINTSTACK(rsp);
            POP
        end
      end
  end
end;

begin {main program}
  BUILDGRAPH;
  FINDALLPATHS
end.
```

Program 13

```
program thirteen(input,output);
type string = packed array[1 . . 10]of char;
     tornt = (t,nt);
     ruleptr = ^rulenode;
     symptr = ^symnode;
     rulenode = record
                     1hs:string;
                     entry:symptr;
                     link:ruleptr
                 end;
     symnode = record
                     alt,link:symptr;
                     case class:tornt of
                     t:(word:string);
                     nt:(rule:ruleptr)
                 end;
var srule,nprule,vprule,nrule,vrule,arule:ruleptr;
    sym1,sym2,sym3,sym4:symptr;
    pno,i,rn:integer;

function RANDOM:integer;
begin
  RANDOM:= rn;
  rn:= (125 * rn + 1)mod 4096
end;

procedure BUILDGRAMMAR;
begin
  new(srule);
  new(nprule);
  new(vprule);
  new(nrule);
  new(vrule);
  new(arule);
  srule^.1hs:= 'sent ';
```

```
srule^.link := nprule;
nprule^.1hs := 'nounphrase';
nprule^.link := vprule;
vprule^.1hs := 'verbphrase';
vprule^.link := nrule;
nrule^.1hs := 'noun ';
nrule^.link := vrule;
vrule^.1hs := 'verb ';
vrule^.link := arule;
arule^.1hs := 'adjective ';
arule^.link := nil;
new(sym1);
new(sym2);
new(sym3);
new(sym4);
sym1^.class := nt;
sym1^.rule := arule;
sym2^.class := nt;
sym2^.rule := nrule;
sym3^.class := t;
sym3^.word := 'boy ';
sym4^.class := t;
sym4^.word := 'apple ';
sym1^.link := sym2;
sym2^.link := nil;
sym3^.link := nil;
sym4^.link := nil;
sym1^.alt := sym3;
sym2^.alt := nil;
sym3^.alt := sym4;
sym4^.alt := nil;
nrule^.entry := sym1;
new(sym1);
new(sym2);
sym1^.class := nt;
sym1^.rule := nprule;
sym2^.class := nt;
sym2^.rule := vprule;
sym1^.alt := nil;
sym1^.link := sym2;
sym2^.alt := nil;
sym2^.link := nil;
srule^.entry := sym1;
new(sym1);
```

```
      new(sym2);
      sym1^.class := t;
      sym1^.word := 'the ';
      sym2^.class := nt;
      sym2^.rule := nrule;
      sym1^.alt := nil;
      sym1^.link := sym2;
      sym2^.alt := nil;
      sym2^.link := nil;
      nprule^.entry := sym1;
      new(sym1);
      new(sym2);
      sym1^.class := nt;
      sym1^.rule := vrule;
      sym2^.class := nt;
      sym2^.rule := nprule;
      sym1^.alt := nil;
      sym1^.link := sym2;
      sym2^.alt := nil;
      sym2^.link := nil;
      vprule^.entry := sym1;
      new(sym1);
      new(sym2);
      sym1^.class := t;
      sym1^.word := 'ate ';
      sym2^.class := t;
      sym2^.word := 'threw ';
      sym1^.alt := sym2;
      sym1^.link := nil;
      sym2^.alt := nil;
      sym2^.link := nil;
      vrule^.entry := sym1;
      new(sym1);
      new(sym2);
      sym1^.class := t;
      sym1^.word := 'small';
      sym2^.class := t;
      sym2^.word := 'large ';
      sym1^.alt := sym2;
      sym1^.link := nil;
      sym2^.alt := nil;
      sym2^.link := nil;
      arule^.entry := sym1;
   end;
```

```
procedure GENSENTENCE(r:ruleptr);
         ⋮

begin {main program}
   writeln('Input seed');
   readln(rn);
   writeln('How many sentences');
   readln(pno);
   BUILDGRAMMAR;
   for i:= 1 to pno do
   begin
      GENSENTENCE(srule);
      writeln
   end
end.
```

Program 14

```
program fourteen(input,output);
label 99;
var sym:char;

procedure ERROR;
begin
  writeln('Error in expression');
  goto 99
end;

procedure GETSYM;
begin
  sym:=' ';
  while sym = ' 'do read(sym)
end;

procedure EXPRESSION;

  procedure PRIMARY;
  begin
    if sym in ['A'..'Z']then GETSYM
    else
    if sym = '('then
    begin
      GETSYM;
      EXPRESSION;
      if sym ⟨ ⟩')' then ERROR else GETSYM
    end
    else
    ERROR
  end;
```

```
    procedure TERM;
    begin
      PRIMARY;
      while sym in [' * ',' / ']do
      begin
        GETSYM;
        PRIMARY
      end
    end;

begin {expression}
  TERM;
  while sym in [' + ',' - ']do
  begin
    GETSYM;
    TERM
  end
end;

begin {main program}
  GETSYM;
  EXPRESSION;
  if sym ⟨ ⟩ '.' then ERROR;
99:
end.
```

Program 15

```
program fifteen(input,output);
label 99;
type tree = ^node;
    node = record
                op:char;
                left,right:tree
            end;
var root:tree;
    sym:char;

procedure ERROR;
        :

procedure GETSYM;
        :

procedure INORDER(ptr:tree);
        :

procedure PREORDER(ptr:tree);
        :

procedure POSTORDER(ptr:tree);
        :
```

```
function EXPRESSION:tree;
var t,temp:tree;
  function TERM:tree;
  var t,temp:tree;
    function PRIMARY:tree;
    var t:tree;
    begin
      if sym = '('then
      begin
        GETSYM;
        PRIMARY:= EXPRESSION;
        if sym⟨ ⟩')'then ERROR else GETSYM
      end
      else
      if sym in ['A'..'Z']then
      begin
        new(t);
        t^.op:= sym;
        t^.left:= nil;
        t^.right:= nil;
        GETSYM;
        PRIMARY:= t
      end
      else
      ERROR
    end;

begin{TERM}
  t:= PRIMARY;
  while sym in ['*','/ ']do
  begin
    temp:= t;
    new(t);
    t^.op:= sym;
    t^.left:= temp;
    GETSYM;
    t^.right:= PRIMARY
  end;
  TERM:= t
end;
```

```
begin{EXPRESSION}
  t:= TERM;
  while sym in [' +',' -']do
  begin
    temp:= t;
    new(t);
    t^.op:= sym;
    t^.left:= temp;
    GETSYM;
    t^.right:= TERM
  end;
  EXPRESSION:= t
end;

begin {main program}
  root:= nil;
  GETSYM;
  root:= EXPRESSION;
  writeln;
  INORDER(root);
  writeln;
  PREORDER(root);
  writeln;
  POSTORDER(root);
  writeln;
  99:
end.
```

Program 16

```
program sixteen(input,output);
label 99;
type tree = ^node;
    node = record
                op:char;
                left,right:tree
            end;
var root:tree;
    sym:char;

procedure ERROR;
begin
  writeln('Error in expression');
  goto 99
end;

procedure GETSYM;
begin
  sym:= ' ';
  while sym = ' 'do read(sym)
end;

procedure CODEGENERATOR(ptr:tree);
        ⋮

function EXPRESSION:tree;
        ⋮

begin {main program}
  root:= nil;
  GETSYM;
  root:= EXPRESSION;
  writeln;
  CODEGENERATOR(root);
  writeln;
  99:
end.
```

Program 17

```
program seventeen(input,output);
label 99;
type tree = ^node;
    node = record
                data:char;
                left,right:tree
            end;
var root:tree;
    sym:char;
    tempstore:integer;

procedure ERROR;
        ⋮

procedure GETSYM;
        ⋮

procedure CODEGEN(op:char;t:tree);
        ⋮

function EXPRESSION:tree;
        ⋮

begin {main program}
    tempstore:= 0;
    root:= nil;
    GETSYM;
    root:= EXPRESSION;
    writeln;
    CODEGEN('=',root);
    writeln;
    99:
end.
```

Program 18

```
program eighteen(input,output);
label 99;
type tree = ^node;
    node = record
                data:char;
                left,right:tree
            end;
var root:tree;
    sym:char;
    tempstore:integer;
procedure ERROR;
        ⋮

procedure GETSYM;
        ⋮

procedure CODEGEN(op:char;t:tree);
        ⋮

procedure TRANSFORMTREE(ptr:tree);
        ⋮

function EXPRESSION:tree;
        ⋮
```

```
begin {main program}
  tempstore:= 0;
  root:= nil;
  GETSYM;
  root:= EXPRESSION;
  writeln;
  writeln('Code from original tree');
  writeln;
  CODEGEN(' =',root);
  TRANSFORMTREE(root);
  writeln;
  writeln('Code from transformed tree'); writeln;
  CODEGEN(' =',root);
  writeln;
  99:
end.
```

Program 19

```
program nineteen(input,output);
label 99;
type tree = ^node;
     identifiertree = ^idnode;
     idnode = record
                  name:char;
                  value:integer;
                  lbranch,rbranch:identifiertree
              end;
     node = record
                data:char;
                value:integer;
                lbranch,rbranch:tree
            end;
var expression:tree;
    idtree:identifiertree;
    item,sym:char;
    constvalue,value:integer;
    test:boolean;

procedure INITIALIZE;
begin
  idtree:= nil;
  expression:= nil;
  item:= ' ';
  test:= false;
  constvalue:= 0
end;
```

```
procedure ERROR(n:integer);
begin
  writeln('Error',n:1);
  goto 99
end;

procedure GETSYM;
begin
  sym := ' ';
  while sym = ' 'do read(sym)
end;

procedure FINDVALUE(ptr:identifiertree;item:char;var val:integer);
begin
  if ptr^.name = item then val := ptr^.value
  else
  if ptr^.name > item then
  FINDVALUE(ptr^.lbranch,item,val)
  else
  FINDVALUE(ptr^.rbranch,item,val)
end;
```

```
procedure FINDANDINSERT(var ptr:identifiertree;i:char;n:integer);
var temp,find,follow:identifiertree;
begin
   find:= ptr;
   if find = nil then
   begin
      new(temp);
      temp^.name:= i;
      temp^.value:= n;
      temp^.lbranch:= nil;
      temp^.rbranch:= nil;
      ptr:= temp
   end
   else
   begin
      while find< >nil do
      begin
         follow:= find;
         if i = find^.name then ERROR(1)
         else
         if i < find^.name then find:= find^.lbranch
                     else find:= find^.rbranch
      end;
      new(temp);
      if i < follow^.name then follow^.lbranch:= temp
                  else follow^.rbranch:= temp;
      temp^.name:= i;
      temp^.value:= n;
      temp^.lbranch:= nil;
      temp^.rbranch:= nil
   end
end;

procedure READCONST;
begin
   if sym in['A'..'Z']then item:= sym
                  else ERROR(2);
   GETSYM;
   if sym = '=' then read(constvalue)
            else ERROR(3);
   GETSYM
end;
```

```
procedure FINDIDENTIFIER(ptr:identifiertree;i:char;var found:boolean);
begin
  if ptr = nil then found := false
  else
  if ptr^.name = i then found := true
  else
  if ptr^.name > i then
  FINDIDENTIFIER(ptr^.lbranch,i,found)
  else
  FINDIDENTIFIER(ptr^.rbranch,i,found)
end;

function EXPTREE:tree;
var etree,temp:tree;
    op:char;

  function TERMTREE:tree;
  var ttree,temp:tree;
      op:char;

    function PRIMTREE:tree;
    var ptree:tree;
    begin
      if sym in['A'..'Z']then
      begin
        FINDIDENTIFIER(idtree,sym,test);
        if test<>true then ERROR(4)
        else
        begin
          new(ptree);
          ptree^.data := sym;
          ptree^.lbranch := nil;
          ptree^.rbranch := nil;
          PRIMTREE := ptree;
          GETSYM
        end
      end
      else
      if sym = '('then
      begin
        GETSYM;
        PRIMTREE := EXPTREE;
        if sym = ')'then GETSYM
        else ERROR(5)
      end
```

```
        else
        ERROR(6)
      end;

  begin {termtree}
    ttree := PRIMTREE;
    while sym in[' * ',' / ']do
    begin
      op := sym;
      GETSYM;
      temp := ttree;
      new(ttree);
      ttree^.data := op;
      ttree^.lbranch := temp;
      ttree^.rbranch := PRIMTREE
    end;
    TERMTREE := ttree
  end;

begin {exptree}
  if sym = ' − 'then
  begin
    op := '$';
    GETSYM;
    temp := TERMTREE;
    new(etree);
    etree^.data := op;
    etree^.lbranch := nil;
    etree^.rbranch := temp
  end
  else
  etree := TERMTREE;
  while sym in[' + ',' − ']do
  begin
    op := sym;
    GETSYM;
    temp := etree;
    new(etree);
    etree^.data := op;
    etree^.lbranch := temp;
    etree^.rbranch := TERMTREE
  end;
  EXPTREE := etree
end;
```

```
procedure EVALUATE(ptr:tree);
begin
  if ptr⟨ ⟩nil then
  begin
    EVALUATE(ptr^.lbranch);
    EVALUATE(ptr^.rbranch);
    if ptr^.data in['A'..'Z']then
    begin
      FINDVALUE(idtree,ptr^.data,value);
      ptr^.value:= value
    end
    else
    case ptr^.data of
    '+':ptr^.value:= ptr^.lbranch^.value + ptr^.rbranch^.value;
    '-':ptr^.value:= ptr^.lbranch^.value - ptr^.rbranch^.value;
    '*':ptr^.value:= ptr^.lbranch^.value * ptr^.rbranch^.value;
    '/ ':ptr^.value:= ptr^,lbranch^.value div ptr^.rbranch^.value;
    '$':ptr^.value:= - ptr^.rbranch^.value
    end
  end
end;

begin {main program}
  INITIALIZE;
  GETSYM;
  READCONST;
  FINDANDINSERT(idtree,item,constvalue);
  while sym  = ','do
  begin
    GETSYM;
    READCONST;
    FINDANDINSERT(idtree,item,constvalue);
  end;
  while sym  = ';'do
  begin
    GETSYM;
    expression:= EXPTREE;
    EVALUATE(expression);
    writeln('Result ',expression^.value);
    dispose(expression)
  end;
  writeln;
99:
end.
```

Program 20

```
program twenty(input,output);
label 99;
type tree = ^node;
     identifiertree = ^idnode;
     sptr = ^snode;
     iptr = ^inode;
     idnode = record
                 name:char;
                 value:integer;
                 lbranch,rbranch:identifiertree
              end;
     node = record
                data:char;
                value:integer;
                lbranch,rbranch:tree
             end;
     snode = record
                 data:integer;
                 next:sptr
              end;
     inode = record
                 op,oprand:char;
                 next:iptr
              end;

var expression:tree;
    idtree:identifiertree;
    item,sym:char;
    constvalue,value,op1,op2,res:integer;
    test:boolean;
    stackptr:sptr;
    instptr,endptr:iptr;
```

```
procedure INITIALIZE;
begin
  idtree := nil;
  expression := nil;
  item := ' ';
  test := false;
  constvalue := 0;
  stackptr := nil;
  instptr := nil
end;

procedure ERROR(n:integer);
begin
  writeln('Error',n:1);
  goto 99
end;

procedure GETSYM;
begin
  sym := ' ';
  while sym = ' ' do read(sym)
end;

procedure FINDVALUE(ptr:identifiertree;item:char;var val:integer);
begin
  if ptr^.name = item then val := ptr^.value
  else
  if ptr^.name > item then
  FINDVALUE(ptr^.lbranch,item,val)
  else
  FINDVALUE(ptr^.rbranch,item,val)
end;
```

```
procedure FINDANDINSERT(var ptr:identifiertree;i:char;n:integer);
var temp,find,follow:identifiertree;
begin
  find := ptr;
  if find = nil then
  begin
    new(temp);
    temp^.name := i;
    temp^.value := n;
    temp^.lbranch := nil;
    temp^.rbranch := nil;
    ptr := temp
  end
  else
  begin
    while find< >nil do
    begin
      follow := find;
      if i = find^.name then ERROR(1)
      else
      if i < find^.name then find := find^.lbranch
                    else find := find^.rbranch
    end;
    new(temp);
    if i < follow^.name then follow^.lbranch := temp
                else follow^.rbranch := temp;
    temp^.name := i;
    temp^.value := n;
    temp^.lbranch := nil;
    temp^.rbranch := nil
  end
end;

procedure READCONST;
begin
  if sym in['A'..'Z']then item := sym
                else ERROR(2);
  GETSYM;
  if sym = '=' then read(constvalue)
          else ERROR(3);
  GETSYM
end;
```

```
procedure FINDIDENTIFIER(ptr:identifiertree;i:char;var found:boolean);
begin
   if ptr = nil then found := false
   else
   if ptr^.name = i then found := true
   else
   if ptr^.name > i then
   FINDIDENTIFIER(ptr^.lbranch,i,found)
   else
   FINDIDENTIFIER(ptr^.rbranch,i,found)
end;

   function EXPTREE:tree;
   var etree,temp:tree;
       op:char;

      function TERMTREE:tree;
      var ttree,temp:tree;
          op:char;

         function PRIMTREE:tree;
         var ptree:tree;
         begin
           if sym in['A'..'Z']then
           begin
             FINDIDENTIFIER(idtree,sym,test);
             if test< >true then ERROR(2)
             else
             begin
               new(ptree);
               ptree^.data := sym;
               ptree^.lbranch := nil;
               ptree^.rbranch := nil;
               PRIMTREE := ptree;
               GETSYM
             end
           end
           else
           if sym = '('then
           begin
             GETSYM;
             PRIMTREE := EXPTREE;
             if sym = ')'then GETSYM
             else ERROR(5)
           end
```

```
            else
            ERROR(6)
         end;

      begin {termtree}
         ttree:= PRIMTREE;
         while sym in[' * ','/ ']do
         begin
            op:= sym;
            GETSYM;
            temp:= ttree;
            new(ttree);
            ttree^.data:= op;
            ttree^.lbranch:= temp;
            ttree^.rbranch:= PRIMTREE
         end;
         TERMTREE:= ttree
      end;

      begin {exptree}
         etree:= TERMTREE;
         while sym in[' +','- ']do
         begin
            op:= sym;
            GETSYM;
            temp:= etree;
            new(etree);
            etree^.data:= op;
            etree^.lbranch:= temp;
            etree^.rbranch:= TERMTREE
         end;
         EXPTREE:= etree
      end;
procedure POP(var ptr:sptr;var item:integer);
var temp:sptr;
begin
   if ptr⟨ ⟩ nil then
   begin
      item:= ptr^.data;
      temp:= ptr;
      ptr:= ptr^.next;
      dispose(temp)
   end
end;
```

```
procedure STACKCODE(ptr;tree;var cptr:iptr);
var codeptr:iptr;
begin
  if ptr⟨ ⟩nil then
  begin
    STACKCODE(ptr^.lbranch,cptr);
    STACKCODE(ptr^.rbranch,cptr);
    new(codeptr);
    codeptr^.next:= nil;
    if ptr^.data in ['A'..'Z']then codeptr^.op:= 'L'
    else codeptr^.op:= 'A';
    codeptr^.oprand:= ptr^.data;
    if cptr = nil then
    begin
      cptr:= codeptr;
      endptr:= codeptr
    end
    else
    begin
      endptr^.next:= codeptr;
      endptr:= codeptr
    end
  end
end;

procedure WRITECODE(ptr:iptr);
begin
  while ptr⟨ ⟩nil do
  begin
    if ptr^.op = 'L'then writeln('LOAD ',ptr^.oprand)
    else writeln('APPLY ',ptr^.oprand);
    ptr:= ptr^.next
  end
end;
```

```
procedure INTERPRET(ptr:iptr);
var stackelement:sptr;
begin
   while ptr〈〉nil do
   begin
   case ptr^.op of
   'L':begin
         FINDVALUE(idtree,ptr^.oprand,value);
         new(stackelement);
         stackelement^.data := value;
         stackelement^.next := stackptr;
         stackptr := stackelement
      end;
   'A':begin
         POP(stackptr,op1);
         POP(stackptr,op2);
         case ptr^.oprand of
         '+':res := op2+op1;
         '−':res := op2−op1;
         '*':res := op2*op1;
         '/':res := op2 div op1
         end;
         new(stackelement);
         stackelement^.data := res;
         stackelement^.next := stackptr;
         stackptr := stackelement
      end
   end;
   ptr := ptr^.next
   end
end;
```

```
begin {main program}
  INITIALIZE;
  GETSYM;
  READCONST;
  FINDANDINSERT(idtree,item,constvalue);
  while sym  = ','do
  begin
    GETSYM;
    READCONST;
    FINDANDINSERT(idtree,item,constvalue);
  end;
  while sym  = ';'do
  begin
    GETSYM;
    expression:= EXPTREE;
    writeln;
    STACKCODE(expression,instptr);
    WRITECODE(instptr);
    writeln;
    INTERPRET(instptr);
    writeln('Result ',stackptr^.data);
    expression:= nil;
    instptr:= nil;
    stackptr:= nil
  end;
  writeln;
99:
end.
```

Glossary

accumulator A special purpose register in a microprocessor used for holding the values of expressions and subexpressions.

adjacency lists One method of recording data about a graph. Each vertex is listed together with a list of its adjacent vertices.

ambiguous A term applied to a grammar. An ambiguous grammar is capable of giving different phrase structures (meanings) to the same sentence.

ancestors All of the predecessor nodes to a given node in some suitably defined data structure, i.e. a family tree.

array A data structure designed to hold many individual elements of the same type but accessed through a single identifier.

array identifier The name given to a contiguous block of storage cells used to store array elements.

atom A single element in a list that is itself not a list.

Backus Naur form A notation used for defining the syntax of a programming language.

BASIC A high level programming language. There are many non-compatible versions in use.

binary operator An operator that requires two operands.

binary tree A tree data structure in which each node is restricted to having zero, one or two branches to successor nodes. If the restriction is such that only zero or two branches to successor nodes are allowed then the structure is called a strict binary tree.

branch node The internal nodes of a tree structure; i.e. a branch node has both predecessor and successor nodes.

commutative A term applied to arithmetic operators whose order of operands does not affect the result; i.e. $3 + 4$ gives the same result as $4 + 3$, therefore $+$ is said to be a commutative operator.

compiler A language translator specifically designed to translate statements from a high level programming language to a lower level, assembler-type language or to intermediate code.

constructor function A function that operates on lists. Normally takes an item and appends it to a list, thus constructing a new list.

contiguous A term which denotes a block of adjacent storage cells in computer memory.

critical activities The activities represented by those arcs that form a critical path through a graph.

critical path The longest path through a graph from source vertex to destination vertex when each arc represents an activity measured in time.

derivation tree The tree structure produced when applying the rules of a grammar to derive a given sentence.

destination vertex The vertex reached by following a given path through a graph.

directed graph A graph in which the arcs connecting the vertices can be transversed in one direction only. This direction is normally indicated by an arrow on the arc.

dispose A Pascal function for returning unwanted storage to the heap.

dot notation A method used for addressing the different fields of a Pascal record.

dynamic storage Computer memory cells which are allocated and deallocated during the execution of a program.

edges The lines or arcs that connect the vertices of a graph.

element A member of a set of objects; i.e. Monday is an element of the set of weekdays.

expression tree A tree structure that represents the phrase structure (meaning) of an algebraic/arithmetic expression.

Fibonacci An infinite sequence of integers starting with 1 and 1 and such that any member of the sequence is equal to the sum of its two predecessors, i.e. 1,1,2,3,5,8,13,.....

field A named part of a Pascal record structure.

grammar The set of rules or productions defining the syntax of a programming language.

graph A set of vertices connected by edges or arcs where each arc represents some particular relationship between vertices.

head The first node in a linear data structure. All other nodes in the structure are accessible only through the head node.

heap An area of storage reserved for use by the Pascal functions NEW and DISPOSE, thus allowing the dynamic use of storage cells.

identifier The name associated with a single or with a group of storage cells.

index notation A method used to identify individual elements of an array; i.e. if the array identifier is X then (i) refers to the ith element of the array.

infix notation A notational device commonly used in algebraic/arithmetic expressions where each binary operator appears between its operands, e.g. $A + B$.

in-order traverse A particular way of visiting each node of a tree structure. If the tree structure represents an algebraic expression then writing down the data contents of each node during such a traverse gives the infix form of the expression.

integer Any of the infinite set of numbers $\ldots -3, -2, -1, 0, 1, 2, 3, \ldots$.

intermediate code Code generated by a compiler for execution on some hypothetical computer. In Pascal implementations this intermediate code is referred to as P.code.

interpreter A system that normally executes intermediate or compiled code.

leaf A node in a tree structure that has no successor nodes (a terminal node).

left grouping In an arithmetic/algebraic expression, if all the operators are of equal precedence, evaluation is carried out from left to right; $3 + 4 + 5 - 6$ implies left grouping viz. $(((3 + 4) + 5) - 6)$.

linear data structure A set of similar-type items connected in a linear sequence.

link The connection between items in a linked data structure. Normally the memory address of the next item.

linked system A storage system in which each storage cell is connected to the next available cell by a link, thus obviating the need for contiguous locations. However, one of the penalties of a linked system is that more physical storage is needed.

mapping function A function used by computer systems to evaluate the address of a given storage cell when referenced in a program by means of the index notation.

menu driven A program that presents the user with a list of choices and branches according to the user choice. After executing each choice the program loops back to display the menu again.

metalinguistic Refers to the symbols of a metalanguage; e.g. the pointed brackets in BNF notation are metalinguistic symbols as they are not part of the language being defined.

new A Pascal function used to obtain dynamic variables from the heap.

nil The value given to a pointer (link) in order to indicate that it points nowhere. The last link of a list must contain a nil pointer.

node An individual item in a linked data structure.

non-linear A data structure in which the nodes are linked together in a non-linear form; i.e. a binary tree is a non-linear structure.

non-terminal Applied to a node in a binary tree implies that it has successor nodes.

non-terminal symbol A symbol in a programming language capable of being further subdivided into terminal and/or non-terminal symbols.

operand The item or items to which an operator is applied.

operator A definition of the action taken on one or more operands.

ordered list A list of items appearing in some predetermined way, i.e. alphabetically or numerically sorted.

partial ordering A directed graph in which there exists no cyclic paths is said to represent a partial ordering.

Pascal A high level, well-structured programming language designed by Professor N. Wirth.

paths Ways of traversing between given vertices in a graph.

phrase structure Gives a unique meaning to the sentences generated by a non-ambiguous grammar.

pointer The address of a memory cell.

polish A form of the prefix functional notation but without parentheses and commas.

postfix A notational device used in algebraic/arithmetic expressions in which each operator is preceded by a parenthesized list of its operands separated by commas, e.g. $(A,B)+$.

post-order traverse See in-order traverse. If the tree structure represents an algebraic expression, writing down the data contents during such a traverse gives the reverse polish form of the expression.

precedence The heirarchy of arithmetic operators. Operator precedence. In Pascal the precedence of operators is as follows:

highest	not
	*,/,div,mod,and
	+,−,or
lowest	=,⟨⟩,⟨,⟩,⟨=,⟩=

prefix A notational device used in algebraic/arithmetic expressions in which each operator precedes a parenthesized list of its operands separated by commas, e.g. $+(A,B)$.

pre-order traverse See in-order traverse. If the tree structure represents an algebraic expression, writing down the data contents of each node during such a traverse gives the polish form of the expression.

processor The heart of a computer. The part that controls the execution of instructions.

PUSH and POP Stack operators. PUSH pushes an element on to the top of a stack while POP removes the top element from a stack.

queue A special type of linear list in which additions are allowed at one end only and deletions are allowed only at the opposite end.

real numbers Any rational or irrational number.

record A single data item whose fields can hold items of differing data types.

recursion The ability of a procedure to refer to and hence call itself.

reverse operator An operator that reverses the order of its operands, i.e. X (reverse $-$) Y means $Y - X$.

reverse polish A form of the postfix functional notation but without parentheses and commas.

root node The first node in a tree structure. All other nodes in the structure are accessible only through this node.

seed A number used to initialize a random number generator function.

selector functions Functions that operate on linear lists. They are used to select individual items from the list.

sentence A string of terminal symbols generated by some grammar.

sentinal node A dummy or additional node added to a data structure to assist in processing.

set difference The difference between SET1 and SET2 is the set that contains those items of SET1 that are not members of SET2.

set equality Two sets are said to be equal if and only if they both have exactly the same elements.

set inclusion SET1 is said to be included in SET2 if and only if SET1 is a proper subset of SET2.

set intersection The intersection of SET1 and SET2 is the set that contains those elements of SET1 that are also elements of SET2.

set union The union of SET1 and SET2 is the set that contains those elements that are members of SET1 or SET2.

sibling Nodes in a tree structure that have the same predecessor node. Equivalent of brothers and sisters in a family tree.

simple type The non-structured or base types predefined in most programming languages, i.e. numbers, characters, booleans, etc.

source vertex The start of any path in a graph.

sparse array An array in which approximately only 10 per cent of elements are non-zero.

stack A special type of linear list in which additions and deletions are allowed at one end only.

static variable A variable declared by the Pascal VAR statement. If such a variable refers to an array then the dimensions of that array cannot be altered during program execution.

subtree Any part of a tree structure that can be obtained by 'cutting' through a single link or branch.

symbol table A table constructed during compilation of a program. This table contains declared identifier names together with their attributes; it is sometimes referred to as an attribute table.

syntax graphs A method used to define the grammar of a programming language. First used to describe the language Pascal.

tail All of that part of a linear list structure following the head or first node.

terminal node A node in a tree structure that has no successor nodes.

terminal symbol A symbol in a programming language incapable of further subdivision.

time slice A method used when simulating dynamic situations. The system model is examined at the end of fixed predetermined time periods to see if any events have occurred. If so, then the system model is updated accordingly.

topological sort A particular method of ordering the vertices of a graph.

undirected A term applied to an arc or an edge in a graph that may be traversed in either direction.

value parameter An actual parameter to a procedure whose value cannot be altered by a call to that procedure.

variable A term applied to an identifier which references a single or a group of storage cells whose contents may be changed during the execution of a program.

vertices The nodes of a graph structure.

Index

Accumulator, 146, 147, 148
Arrays, 4–9
  mapping function, 6
  sparse arrays, 44, 46, 64
Adjacency lists, 93–96, 107, 109, 112
Adjacency matrix, 112–113

Backus Naur Form, 125
Binary trees, 72–92, 110
  (*see also* Trees)

Code generation, 145–159, 163
Compiler, 145, 161, 163–165

Derivation trees, 122–128
Dijkstra algorithm, 139–141
Dispose, 12, 14
Dot notation, 7, 14
Dynamic storage, 8

Evaluation machines, 144–159
  register-based, 146–150
  stack-based, 145–146, 147, 163, 164
Expressions:
  definition, 125, 130
  evaluation of, 42–44, 131, 143–153, 160
  language of, 125
  reordering, 152–159
Expression trees, 131–139, 142–143, 149–157, 161
  building, 135–139
  transformation, 154–159
  traversal, 134–135

Fibonacci series, 20

Grammar, 117–121,
  ambiguous grammar, 127
  building grammar, 120, 121

grammar rules, 117–121
  representation, 118–121
Graphs, 92–110,
  activities, 103–105
  building graphs, 95–96
  critical activities, 104, 105
  critical paths, 104, 105
  directed, 92, 102, 112
  precedence relationships, 101

Identifier tree, 161, 164
Infix notation, 132, 134, 139
Instruction generation
  (*see* Code generation), intermediate
  code, 125
Interpreter, 161–163

Language generation, 117–122
Left grouping, 43
Linked lists:
  building lists, 15, 28
  circular lists, 31
  doubly linked lists, 31
  generalized lists, 59
  length, 21
  node deletion, 24–30
  node insertion, 23–30
  ordered lists, 25, 28
  reversing, 49–50
  searching, 18, 22–23
  sentinel nodes, 28–30
  writing lists, 18
List functions:
  constructor, 48–49
  head, 47, 48
  tail, 48

Metalinguistic symbols, 125

New, 12, 13, 17

Nil link, 8
Non-terminal symbols, 117
number base conversion, 41–42

Ordered pairs, 96

Partial ordering, 96, 101
Phrase structure, 123, 156
Pointers, 9
Polish notation, 134
Pool/heap storage, 8–12, 73,
  getting a node, 9, 12
  initialization, 12
  returning a node, 10, 12
POP, 38, 40
Postfix notation, 133, 134
Prefix notation, 133, 134
Primary definition, 125, 131
PUSH, 38–40

Queue, 34–37

Random number generator, 36
Records, 6–13, 60,
  tag fields, 60
  variant records, 60
Recursion, 19–22, 118
Reverse polish notation, 134, 139, 142,
  143

Sentence generation, 121, 122
Sets, 50–58
  difference, 57–58
  equality, 55–56
  inclusion, 56–57
  intersection, 51–52
  membership, 55
  ordered sets, 50–55
  union, 52–55
Stack, 38–44, 64, 139, 142–144, 165

Stack based evaluation, 145–146,
  163–165
Subtree, 70
Symbol table, 147
Syntax, 117, 123, 131
Syntax analysis, 130–131, 137
Syntax errors, 124
Syntax graphs, 128–130, 135–137

Term definition, 125, 131
Terminal symbols, 117, 125
Time-slice, 34
Topological sorting, 96–98, 101, 102
Trees, 70–92
  balanced trees, 112
  binary trees, 72–92, 110
  binary search tree, 74, 110, 161
  branch nodes, 72, 74
  building trees, 75
  degree, 71
  deleting nodes, 78–82
  inserting nodes, 75–78
  leaf/terminal nodes, 71, 74
  ordered tree, 73
  proper subtree, 123
  representation, 73–74
  root node, 71, 74
  searching, 76
Tree traversal, 82–92
  in-order, 83–85
  post-order, 86–89
  pre-order, 85–86
Tuples/triples, 46–47, 64
Type, 7, 8, 13

Variables, identifiers, 3, 4, 13, 145
  BASIC, 3
  global, 64, 150
  local, 64
  PASCAL, 4, 5